MW01628875

Fly Fishing, the Book Series, Volume Two:

Reading Waters

Fly Fishing, the Book Series, Volume Two:

Reading Waters

Gary A. Borger

Illustrations & Additional Text
by Jason Borger

READING WATERS

First Printing

Published by:

TOMORROW RIVER PRESS
P.O. Box 1745
Wausau, WI 54402-1745

Library of Congress Control Number: 2010943406

ISBN 978-0-9628392-8-3

Printed in the U.S.A.

Front and back cover photos by Gary Borger.

For my Brother (Rom. 8:17)

And for Nancy
best friend, wife, fellow fisher, and selfless companion
in reading the waters of life

Table of Contents

Acknowledgments

No author fishes in the book pool alone. Every book is a multi-faceted, cooperative effort between author, editor, illustrator, designer, publisher, and printer. For Jason and me this book project has been an opportunity to work together and exchange insights on the whole of fly fishing.

Further, I want to acknowledge Jason's many hours slaving over hot pixels to get this book edited, illustrated, assembled, and put to bed. Your efforts are deeply appreciated!

As this project has developed, I've had the unflinching steadfastness of my wife, Nancy, supporting me as I've burned the midnight oil or used up a Saturday and Sunday that we could have spent in family time. Nancy has figured heavily in many of the experiences in these books because she has been with me, fishing, much of the time. Furthermore, she served as another "set of eyes," offering solid commentary and needed edits of the final text. Thanks, Nanc.

Dr. Henry Kanemoto read early drafts and gave me useful comments that helped guide the final text to completion. Thanks, Henry.

Of course, I must say thanks, too, to the staff at BookMasters, who were so helpful with all the little details involved in finalizing the book for printing and distribution.

Editor's Preface

About the Book

This book is titled *Reading Waters*, which is a topic that has wide-ranging angling implications. Reading water is much more than just surveying currents or structure in order to find likely holding spots for fish. Reading water is really a holistic strategy that combines a number of individual elements into a bigger angling picture.

In this book you will find explanations of the fish's three lies and how to identify them in all water types. You will also find a wide-ranging discussion that explores the concepts of fish location and angling approach in flowing waters and stillwaters (often within the context of "example" waters), including a look at ocean flats. Within that larger picture are details of specific water features, such as riffles, pools, rapids, runs, flats, the secret river, and more. And, of course, there are stories that bring personalized illumination to the whole process of reading waters.

About the Series

"It's all related."

Fly fishing, that is. Freshwater, saltwater, single-handed, double-handed, trout, tarpon, it all comes back to a love of the fly, and ultimately a way of making the illusion seem real. This book series is much the same. It will explore many facets of the art/sport of fly fishing, but in the end it's about making our offerings appear believable.

One interesting thing about that central tenet of our art/sport is that there really is so much that overlaps, so many skills and ideas and approaches that bleed together in similarity. Fly fishing can sometimes seem very compartmentalized and specialized, with each type and subtype (and subtypes of the subtypes) being awash in their own exclusive lexicon. But when we strip away the confines that we sometimes place on our mind-sets, there is an underlying, interlaced flow revealed.

Some of the examples and stories woven into these books may appear several times throughout the series. This isn't a thinly veiled attempt to recycle a few words; rather it's a way to view the same angling situation from different perspectives. A story may be able to teach one thing when looked at a certain way, but it may teach another when one's gaze comes from an alternate direction. A story on tarpon fishing, for example, may teach something about casting, but it may also teach something about fishing the film and about fighting fish. We feel that viewing an angling experience in more than one dimension helps to better interconnect the various aspects of fly fishing across seemingly different backdrops.

Retaining coherence across the series is a big part of the task—to keep the books linked and speaking through one another, and ultimately to express those relationships to you, the reader. At the same time, the books are designed to stand on their own, without the need for additional support to accomplish their teaching tasks. While the series as a whole will allow for the greatest scope of reference and related ideas, each book should allow you to engage deeply in the individual topic at hand.

The ultimate goal with this series is to make something of lasting value—a library of thoughts and experiences that create a useful reference and teaching tool. Enjoy the read!

Jason Borger
Series Editor, illustrator and contributor

Note: For a listing of all of the books in this series, see the section entitled "The Books of the 'Fly Fishing' Series" just prior to the Index.

Reading Waters

Waters have always held a fascination for me. Among the dimness of my first memories are stories of my mother and father going fishing for spring suckers the day before I was born. It was during the War, and they had little except each other and the few enjoyments that nature offered. The bouquets that graced the family table were from the field, not the florist, and the meat was often wild game, not domestic. Clothes were very much hand-me-down, or from the box at church. There was no television, no computers, no video games, only the things that a wild imagination could conjure out of sticks and stones and other items from nature.

We had a rough and tumble childhood, and my mother's constant plea was to, "Go outside to play." And play we did. But there were also the times when we would hike through the pasture to find ourselves on the banks of Beatty Run, where we would fish and wade in the water for hours on end. We built stone dams, we erected forts by the stream, we made "fish traps" that trapped exactly nothing. But all the while, waters were flowing ever more strongly in my life.

My older brother, Val, and I were permitted to go to the "big" stream, Sugar Creek, when I was about six. In fact, my first solo camping trip was in the spring of my sixth birthday. I chose to camp on the very spot where my parents had fished for suckers those six years before, and I too soaked worms in hopes of catching suckers in the roily waters of spring. Late that night it poured rain, and when my father came looking for me—at my mother's instance in the middle of the night—my dogs kept him at bay until I awoke and called them off.

My connection to waters will always be with me.

Waters were a constant in our lives. We swam in the creeks, we fished for trout, we speared suckers, and we hunted bullfrogs with our bows. No one taught us to read waters, we just grew up in them and came to know their character by the feel of them against bare skin, by the look of them as they ran high in spring, leaving detritus in the branches higher than our heads, and by their beckoning gurgle as they slid past in the night. It was idyllic, but it was also a connection to waters that will always be with me.

When we as fly fishers think of reading waters, it is usually with the sole intent of finding a fish that will rise to the fly. But there's so much more there to see, and that needs to be seen. From the strictly utilitarian viewpoint, there's the need to interpret currents so that we can select he best cast and mend, pick the right fly, so that we know where fish hide, where they are likely to be feeding, and how best to hook, fight and land them. Reading waters is not always easy, and it's not always cut and dry—it is *water* after all.

Mark of the Payara

All fishing is inter-related. What one knows about one species can be transferred to other species. What one knows about reading waters in one stream can be transferred to another stream. Or so I always thought. But this occasion was very much different. This was not a trout stream, it wasn't even a stream. It could never be called anything but a river, a "super-river." The Orinoco is a massive flow of water that comes out of the high ground on the northern edge of the Amazonian basin and sweeps north and east to the Caribbean Sea. Just seeing it instills in one an overwhelming sense of sheer, unstoppable power. From where I stood, it was a mile and half to the far shore; there, howler monkeys set up their jet engine roars. The water, thirty feet deep in the shallows, seemed to fight itself to see which current would be first to taste the salt.

Ed Rice and I were there to fish for payara. Little exploited by the fly fisher, this species was a new experience for all involved. Our host, guide, and angling companion, Carlos Aristeguieta, had given us a few details, and asked if we would help figure out the best tactics and flies to take these prehistoric looking fish. We came well-equipped, but one look at that water gave us pause. Not to worry, Carlos reassured us, we would start on the small waters. The Caura, a tributary to the Orinoco was merely a half mile wide—a lot easier to cast across! We didn't even hesitate. Out came the 10-weight rods, and on went the forty-foot, lead-core heads backed by 25-pound Amnesia. Also, on went the wire tippets and the biggest flies we could find. When those weren't big enough, we spent the evenings tying even bigger ones.

We started in the places where Carlos knew payara would be holding—faster water stretches where baitfish would be packed in tight against the banks. I use the term baitfish loosely, they were really just smaller fish in the 8 to 18-inch lengths. We'd pound down the banks, heaving with all we had to get the line in tight against the shore, aiming for the shallow spots that were "only" 10 to 15 feet deep. When the fly had gone down for several seconds, we'd rip it back with long pulls, short pulls, medium pulls and every other tactic we could think of. Some spots seemingly held nothing, while other spots gave up several big fish.

Below: Ed Rice fishing for payara on the mighty Orinoco. It can only be called a "super-river."

Drifting down to the Orinoco, we found ourselves in the throws of a rapids—at least it would have been a rapids if the water had not been thirty feet deep. It was a powerful current to say the least, and it swept most impressively along the face of a huge wall of hardpan (densely compacted clay). The standing waves in the swift water were several feet high, and we clung to the bobbing boat with both legs tightly wrapped around the stems of our casting stools. The payara were there, tight against the bank. Any place where there was a protuberance in the cliff wall, or a tree hanging head down in the water, or a boulder pushing above the surface, there were payara.

It was definitely rapid-fire casting. The first heave had to be right because there was no second chance. If the fly dropped in the slot, a payara would meet it with such violence that many times one would forget to strike. Not that there was a need anyway. The heavy line in the heavy current would jam the hook home and the fish would streak out of cover. As soon as a fish was hooked, the other angler would reel in and simply wait out the fight, as the boat was maneuvered downstream into a softer current where the beast could be netted. The payara were released with the much-appreciated help of 12-inch-long, needle-nose pliers.

On the run back to camp later that evening, Ed and I were watching for other such places on the Caura. Seeing a high hardpan bank, we asked Carlos to maneuver the boat so we could cast along it. Coming close, we noticed a series of curved marks on the clay two to four feet above the surface.

"The payara are here," Carlos yelled excitedly. We saw nothing. No fish breaking the surface, not even any impressive holding spots along the bank. So of course, we had our doubts.

"What do you mean?" I asked, not just wanting to know how he could tell such a thing, but also wanting to catch a couple more before darkness drove us off the river.

"The marks on the wall," Carlos pointed excitedly. "Those are wet marks left by the baitfish as they jump out of the water to escape the payara."

My line was in the air before he finished his sentence, and sure enough, the payara were there, and they were nasty hungry. For the rest of the week, we never passed a clay bank without checking to see if it held the mark of the payara.

Reading waters is not always reading waters.

Tigers in the Kalahari

It's the fourth longest river in southern Africa, and also one of the strangest. It starts nearly a thousand miles away in the deep forestlands of Angola and flows southeast into Botswana. There it forms the immensely rich Okavango Delta before evaporating under the withering heat of the Kalahari desert. In the dry season, there is no outlet for the river. There is no lake nor stream to drain away the waters of this, the world's largest inland delta. It just runs out into the desert until it runs no more.

But upstream from its evaporative demise, the Okavango is very much a strong running river filled with a wide variety of fish, including the wild and unpredictable tigerfish. Built like a striper on steroids with teeth like a shark, the tigerfish is the pinnacle of piscatorial predatorship. Its teeth protrude from its mouth and interdigitate, the razor sharp edges sliding past one another. They don't tear bait apart, they slice it to bits.

It was another exploratory trip. Nancy and I were with Ed and Darlene Rice and Charlie and Diane Meyers, fishing three different locations in Botswana, Zimbabwe, and Namibia to evaluate their potential as fishing safari venues. The Okavango was our second location, and we stayed at the comfortable Nxamaseri Camp. At that point, the Okavango is merely a "U" shaped channel in the sand. The banks are heavily overgrown with papyrus, which drapes itself ten to twenty feet out over the water. One can, with a careful study of the rivers' subtleties, discern deeper pools and the occasional underwater sand bar, but much of it looks like the prized project of an agricultural ditch digger.

It was November, the end of the dry season, and smoke from numerous wildfires hung heavily in the air. A blood-red sun greeted our first foray onto the water. As we motored out of the channel from the camp and onto the main river, out host and guide, Jeff Rann, began scanning the horizon for birds. When we entered the confluence pool, Jeff turned the barge down-river and suddenly opened the big engines to full throttle.

Jeff had seen birds heading down-river to a point several miles below camp. After a quick ride, he cut the engines, and we drifted quietly in the currents.

"They'll be coming soon," Jeff said, and we rigged as fast as we could. Single strand wire tippets of 25 to 30 pound test were mandatory, and I attached a big bucktail with a haywire twist, being careful that the turns were as precise as I could make them. I didn't want to lose the fly, nor the fish that I was certain would take it.

Then we heard them. A school of barbel—an African catfish—was headed our way. Stretching for over a half mile, the school contained thousands upon thousands of fish. They moved up the river slowly, working along the edge, back under the papyrus. Occasionally they showed at the edge of the vegetation. The sound they made was totally unique: a slurping, splashing, sucking sound that could be heard from hundreds of yards away. The birds were there, too. They were in the papyrus above the big school, flapping down to grab baitfish as they rolled, jumped and flopped to escape the barbel.

The razor sharp teeth of the tigerfish make it a formidable predator.

And then we saw them. They were on the outside of the school of barbel, waiting for the baitfish that spooked out into open water. The slashes and powerful swirling grabs were tigers. They were the outriders on the herd, watching for strays, which they immediately rounded up and devoured. The trick was to control one's desire to just cast and strip. We waited until a fish was clearly spotted by its slashing rise. Then the fly was immediately presented, as close to the fish as possible. The tigers were moving fast, and if the cast was delayed, the fish would be long gone. Like the payara that Ed Rice and I caught in South America, these fish were released with the help of 12-inch-long needle-nosed pliers.

Reading waters is not always reading waters.

First Bonefish

My focus has always been on trout. I'm not really certain why. Perhaps it is because I grew up near trout waters, and they are so ingrained in my youthful memories. Perhaps it was the long-ago stories spun by the likes of Brooks and Trueblood, Schwiebert and McClane. Perhaps it has been in the unraveling of the mysteries that surround trout, and the tying of the multitude of patterns that are used in search of them. In any case, although trout are still my first love, I have no aversion to fishing for anything that swims, especially when I can sight fish for them.

So when John Pinto called and invited me on an exploratory trip to the Bahamas in search of new bonefish waters, I grabbed the sunscreen and headed for the airport. John had been an instructor in my fly fishing schools for many years, but had given up trout for bones, tarpon, permit, and other flats fish. He just liked the warmer waters and the stalking of individual fish that the flats offered. As we traveled to our destination, John held a running conversation on the virtues of fishing the flats, and all the tactics that one had to understand if they were to be successful as a bonefisher.

To me, it all sounded exactly like fishing for big trout in the razor thin waters of the big lakes in New Zealand, the high country lakes of the Vermejo Ranch in New Mexico, the reservoirs in England, the spring ponds of Wisconsin, and a hundred other places I had been blessed to fish over the years. But I kept quiet, remembering the old saying, "Open mouth, insert foot." I didn't want to appear overly confident on one side or a total neophyte on the other. So, I just sat back and listened. John was enthusiastic, and it's always fun to listen to someone who gets so pumped up over fishing.

There were no lodges on the island, and we stayed at a private home that offered a couple of rooms for rent. There were no boats on the island except a small canoe that John had sent ahead on the mail boat. We set up our gear before we launched. The tide was moving in, and conditions were absolutely ideal—no wind, a gently flowing tide, and big flats stretching off into the distance. We hopped aboard the canoe and paddled across the deep channel to the edge of the first flat.

"Watch closely," John cautioned, "Bones can be really hard to see, and they're really spooky."

"You mean like those over there?" I replied as casually as possible. A series of tails was sticking above the surface about 80 yards away, and I was already climbing out of the canoe after them.

The tails made the approach easy. When I was about 60 feet away, I stopped and watched. Two nice fish were quartering toward me. I pitched the unweighted Boggle Head about 20 feet ahead of them and let it sink to the bottom. When it looked like they were on it, I gave a short strip. The first fish covered the fly instantly, and I stripped once more to "feel for the fish." It was there, and the strip stuck the hook home.

The seven-pound bone fought like a seven-pound, New Zealand brown hooked in razor thin water on 5X. It was my first bonefish, and it had struck like clockwork.

Reading waters is not always reading waters.

Below: Fishing the flats is often more about seeing fish than simply "reading waters."

Spooled

Alaska's Newhalen roars through its gorge and practically jumps out into its estuary-like mouth a few miles upstream from Lake Iliamna. It gets a huge run of sockeye headed upstream to spawn in the tributaries of Lake Clark. They congregate in the monster reverse currents set up at the sides of the cascading main river where it pours out of the canyon. If there are sockeyes in such numbers, there are certainly sockeye eggs. And, if there are sockeye eggs, there are trout—big rainbows up from Iliamna.

I was staying at Iliamna Lake Lodge, and was fishing both the local and fly-out waters, as the weather permitted. This day, the clouds had come in and draped the big lake and surrounding hills with an impenetrable white fog. So it was off to the Newhalen. I stood on the hill overlooking the river, and spent a few minutes just watching and thinking. It seemed to me that the trout would be in the seam between the reverse and the main current. There, sockeye eggs would be concentrated, and easy to nibble on as they drifted along.

I had developed my favored Strip Leech pattern several years before, and I wanted to see what the trout would do with the silver variation. I knotted one to the end of my 12-pound tippet and waded in. I worked upstream toward the reverse current, wading deep and casting long. The currents were powerful, but the big rainbows that nailed the fly were even more powerful. They looked like ocean-fresh steelhead. There was just the faintest hint of pink on the gill plates, with steel-colored backs and heads, and chrome sides. Only later did I realize that the big 'bows of the late season were feasting on the rotting flesh of the sockeyes, and my Silver Leech made a good "flesh fly."

After some time, I finally reached the bottom of the big reverse. It was a bit more than I had anticipated. From high on the hill, it had looked easy to wade, but there, from the perspective of the water itself, it was a dangerous place. I propped myself up against the current, anchoring my feet on the fractured bedrock and gripped my wading staff firmly. This was going to be tricky. I let go of the staff, and chucked the Leech long and hard to reach the seam. The fly drifted about five feet, and the line snapped tight. Startled, I hit the fish hard, and felt it surge off like a torpedo, straight across the violent currents and through the six-foot high standing waves .

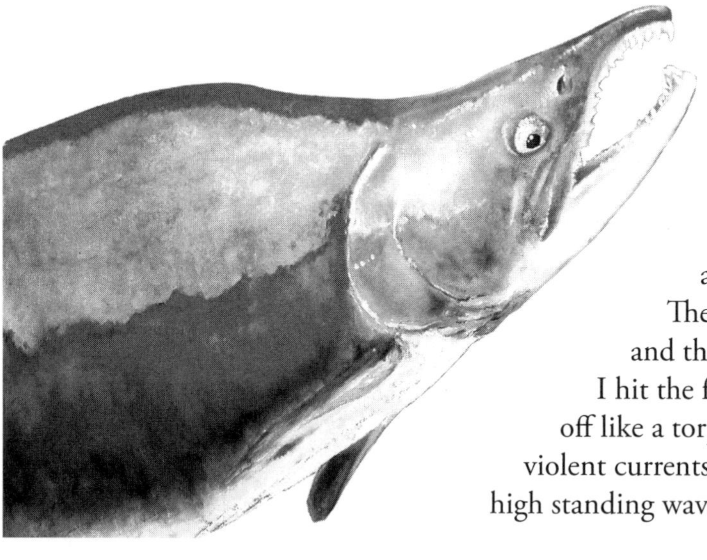

The big rainbows, fresh up from Lake Iliamna, looked very much like steelhead.

The reel played a rather fast flamenco flourish as the fish tore off yard after yard of line. I had spooled on 200 yards of backing with the smug confidence that no Alaskan fish would run that far before I had a chance to run after it. Well, guess what? There would be no running from this precarious place at the edge of the maelstrom. I just held the rod as high as possible, and let the fish have its way with me. And it did. Somewhere out there, its head jerked around momentarily as the backing came tight against the reel spool. The leader parted. I'd been spooled and left with a lot of line to reel in.

In my desire to get to "the spot," I had not thought about fighting, playing, and landing anything I might hook there.

Reading waters is not always about finding fish.

The Four-Foot Rod

Jason and I were conducting a nymphing school on Montana's Bighorn, and I had brought along a handful of "test" rods—experimental designs that showed promise but needed water-time. This day, I had a two-piece, 8 1/2 foot, 5-weight that was as light as a feather in the hand and that could toss line into the next county. It was a brilliant rod, and I fished hard all day with nary a wobble or wiggle from it. Wow, I was impressed.

Then, in mid-afternoon, one of the students asked me to demonstrate a technique that I had explained to the group the night before. I wanted to show off a bit with this "test" rod, so I laid out most of the line, and after the drift, let the line swing downstream. It caught a big chunk of floating weeds, and I gave a heave to free the fly. The rod broke cleanly just above the ferrule. The student was shocked, but I told him not to worry, it was a test rod, and it had just failed the torture part of the test.

But, in violation of my own backup procedures, I had not brought another rod on the drift that day. It was time for some creative thinking. I pulled the reel off its seat, and searching around in the boat, I found some strapping tape. It was a bit ugly, but when the reel was taped to the butt end of the tip section, it made a passable four-foot rod. Now, what to do with it?

I could cast as far as I wanted, I could even toss curves and a host of mends. But where could I best use this short stick? Then it dawned on me: I needed to hook, play and land the fish, too. So, a big pool offered me the most opportunity. If I could find feeding fish in a big pool, I had every chance of actually being able to land them on the short rod. We were parked at the top of a riffle, so I waded very quietly up along the side of the pool above, watching the near-shore water carefully. There were overhanging bushes and tree branches, and the water was waist deep. It was a great place for big browns. And then, just above an overhanging branch was a ring in the water.

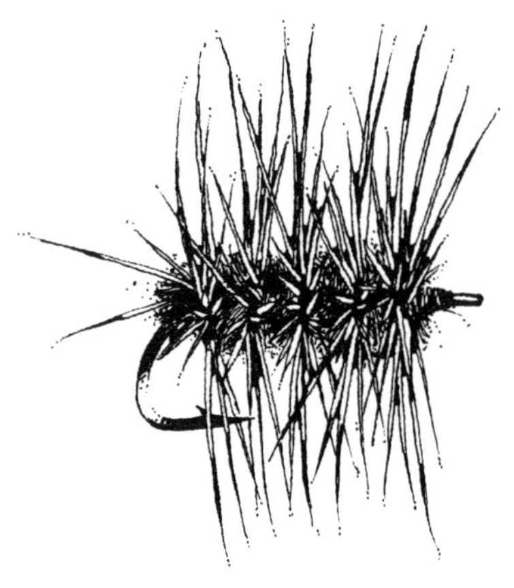

I had already knotted a size 16 Griffith's Gnat to the 5X tippet. Adult midges were swarming around the streamside vegetation, and I chanced that any feeding fish would be eating them. The cast was only about 25 feet, and I added a Curve Mend at the completion of the stroke. The little fly hooked around and fell spot-on, floated about a foot, and disappeared under a big snout. At the set, the fish immediately headed for deep water, but the hook held and soon the trout was mine—all 19 inches of hook-jawed brown. Two more of the big bank feeders took the Griffith's Gnat in the next hour.

Reading waters is not always about finding fish; it may be about selecting the best opportunities.

Rainbows on the Little Danaher

Michigan's Pere Marquette River is a bright little river that sweeps over riffles of fine gravels and small rocks, tucks under cedar sweepers, pushes against high banks, and fills deep, dark pools. Like many of Michigan's waters, there are many springs along its length, and a number of named tributaries, like the Little Danahar, slip their cool waters into its flow. It holds numerous resident browns, and there are runs of salmon and big lake browns in the fall, followed by steelhead in the spring.

Jason and I had conducted fly fishing schools at the Pere Marquette Rod and Gun Club for years. But this year was the first time I had the opportunity to fish the Little Danaher where it joined Danaher Lake. The evening was perfect, as only an early June day can be, and several of us were on the spit of land where the stream dumped into the lake. The question was not where to fish, but what fly to use.

The snail brings success again (and again).

At the confluence of the stream and lake, luxuriant beds of aquatic plants moved slowly in concert with the currents that slowed and spread out into the stillwaters beyond. The weeds suggested something key to me in terms of fly selection. I rummaged through my box and soon had a snail fly clinched to my tippet. I then cast across the stream mouth, allowing the fly to sink slowly and sweep into the waters over the submerged weed beds.

The first take was positive, and the fish fought well, making a good show of itself before being netted. The next cast was a repeat of the first, and then it got really good. The fish came like clockwork, and my companions gathered to watch. But watching only goes so far when there are fish to be had, and my box was soon emptied of all of its snail flies. It ended as a perfect evening of rainbows for all on the Little Danaher.

Reading waters is not always about finding fish; it may well be about fly selection.

A Brown in Reverse

[Text by Jason Borger] With a gloss-black body and multi-hued flames covering its bow, the drift boat looked every bit the part of a '57 Chevy street rod. I figured that with a boat like that, it was going to be a good day even if the fish didn't cooperate. My father, Gary, and I were fishing Montana's Missouri River with our good friend and owner of the Bozeman Angler, Rod King. It was a special occasion for all of us. Because of tight summer schedules, there was only one day when we could all be on the river together, and we had been really looking forward to it.

The float started out right, with a couple of nice browns coming from the weedy, slow water near the put-in. As we moved down-river and came into sight of the mouth of Prickly Pear Creek, our anticipation rose again. There was a huge scum patch at the confluence, and such places often hold a good fish or two. That day was no exception.

We parked the boat and my father headed up to the top end of the huge, slowly revolving sea of foam. Rod and I started along the bottom end. We took our time, partly because we didn't want to miss seeing a feeding fish, but also because it would be way too easy to walk up on a fish and spook it. Suddenly, Rod spotted a movement in the foam and caught my arm. "Right there, Jason," he pointed, and then added, "But he'll be impossible to get in all this foam." Maybe....

Years of stalking cruising trout in shallow lake edges had given me a few clues that I could work with. I figured that the fish likely had a cruising zone staked out, and that even if the fish wasn't following a set circuit, it still had a defined boundary that it was working within. Every ten or twenty seconds, the fish's nose would poke out, and I began to see how that boundary was set. After watching for a few minutes, I could tell approximately where the fish would be, and when. When I felt that the trout was about as close to me as it was going to get, I decided to go for it.

The little nymph threw up a puff of foam as it went in, and I shifted my gaze to the leader. The monofilament was lying on the top of the scum, and I could see it plainly. Suddenly it knifed down through the foam, and I tightened. It was a big brown, and it was right where I had hoped it would be. Rod laughed and shook his head saying, "I don't believe it!"

Frankly, if I hadn't had the opportunity to spend so many years "best guessing" fish in a hundred other places, I wouldn't have believed it either! It's fish like that one that are so incredibly satisfying, but it's also fish like that one that help to reinforce what we learn from our time on the water.

Reading waters is not always about finding fish; it's often about predicting what they'll do once we have found them.

Below: Sometimes reading waters is about predicting fish behavior.

Living in the Lie

Reading waters to locate fish requires that we understand why fish are where fish are. That is, fish are in different places at different times for different reasons. Contrary to some angling lore, fish do not stay put in one place all the time. As a child I was often told that a big brown lived by a particular rock in the stream I fished, and no one could catch it because it was too smart. Boy, did that sucker me in. Being totally naïve in the ways of fish, and as it turned out totally naïve of the way of many anglers, I believed the yarns. But, their stories were not based in fish biology, but were simply myths handed down from generation to generation as angling truth.

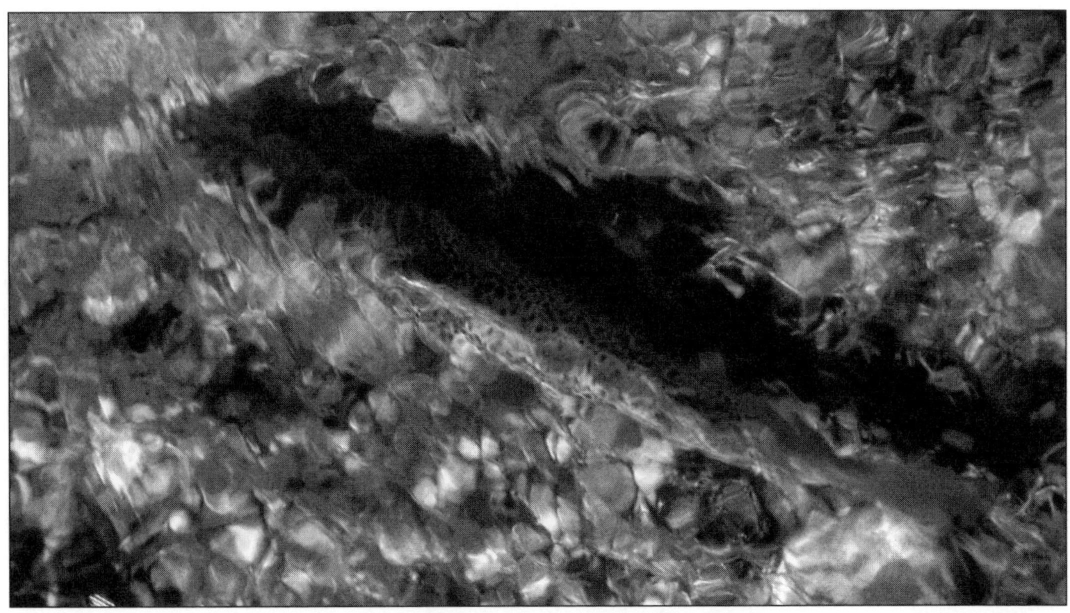

The place that a fish holds in the current is called a "lie."

Most likely a big brown had been seen there once, and because no one could catch it, people assumed that it still lived there, but was just too ancient and too crafty to be caught. The real truth is that the brown easily could have been there once, but had moved on, and no one could catch it because it wasn't there any more. Their assumption had been that once a fish finds a particular spot to occupy it stays put until it dies. That's simply not the case. Fish move around for a variety of reasons: to seek cover, to search for food, to find more suitable water temperatures, for reproduction, and so on.

Studies on the Au Sable River in Michigan, for example, have clearly shown that fish move all over the place for a variety of reasons. One group of big browns lived dispersed in the river during the fall and winter months, but when the hatchery in Grayling opened in the spring, these fish moved several miles up river and lived the rest of the summer in the out-fall pool of the hatchery—eating themselves silly on all the excess trout chow that poured out of the runways. By the way, just so I don't start another myth, the fish did not know when the hatchery opened, but as soon as the chow started coming downstream, they followed it up to the source. In other words, they went in search of more of the great food that was coming down.

Another particularly nice brown spent its days under a mid-stream improvement device, and then at night, moved well over a mile upstream to its feeding grounds. As the sun came up, it headed back to its daytime hide. Other studies on other waters have indicated similar types of diurnal movements.

The up-shot of all this is to point out, quite simply, that fish can be, and often are, in different places at different times for different reasons. Our task, as fly fishers, is to be able to identify the particular places that fish occupy at any given time for each of several reasons, and that is the focus of this chapter (and the rest of the book, for that matter).

Life Rules

All living organisms have three fundamental requirements for life: (1) the need to protect their lives from harm, (2) the desire to seek food to sustain themselves, and (3) the urge to reproduce. From this "must do" list we can derive three life rules.

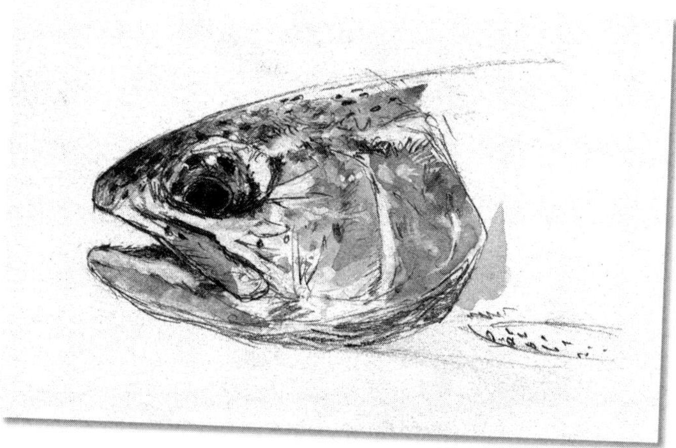

Life Rule #1: Don't Get Eaten!

The primary concern for every organism is survival. Although it is the survival of the species that is at stake, the fate of the individual is critical to this process, because if all the individuals die, the species dies. Thus, the primary drive of every organism is to survive. All animals, even predators, can fall prey to other animals.

So, simply put, Life Rule Number One for all living organisms is "Don't get eaten!" Think about it for a minute. You leave the house on a fine spring morning. You have your favorite sandwich in your lunch bag and hot coffee in the thermos. Life is good. Suddenly, a lion jumps out of the bushes at the end of your driveway and comes roaring at you—and not to get your sandwich, either! What do you do? Do you stop and calmly eat your sandwich because it's the last one you're going to get? Or, do you bolt back to the house, slamming the door shut just as the lion pounces? Once safely inside, do you then calmly sit down and eat your sandwich to celebrate the fact that you've narrowly escaped becoming a lion's lunch? Hardly.

When the adrenaline gets pumping, the desire to eat simply vanishes. When danger threatens, animals go into what is called "fight or flight" mode. This is an adrenaline surge that sets them up to either stand and battle it out with the predator or to get out of there as fast as possible. Once the predator is chased off, or the animal makes it to its hidey-hole, the adrenaline is still surging away. It takes quite a while for the effect of the "fight or flight" reaction to subside.

Or, suppose you're driving on a country road and you crest a hill and see a car in your lane, passing another vehicle. Believe me, the "fight or flight" reaction will kick in instantly. You'll immediately aim for the shoulder to avoid a head-on collision. Once the danger has passed, will you cheerfully wave at the other driver and continue merrily on your way? Doubtful.

It's the same way with a wild fish. They do not wait around to see if the fluorescent orange string and shiny leader flicking back and forth over their heads are going to harm them or are just the accouterments of another silly fly fisher. There are only two kinds of fish—the quick and the dead. The first instinct is to preserve one's skin. Food and reproduction come in a distant second and third.

Life Rule #2: Eat!

Life Rule Number Two is also very simple: "Eat!" *All living organisms require energy to sustain the machinery of life.* Plants harvest their energy from the sun, using it in the photosynthetic process to first produce sugars, and then from the sugars, to make all the other organic molecules they need. Animals eat plants or other animals to get the energy and organic molecules stored in their food organisms. A study of life is, quite simply, a study of energy flow.

Rings on the water. Fish doing everything they can to satisfy Life Rule #2.

The life formula is very simple: **Live or Die = Energy in minus Energy out**. If more energy goes in than goes out, the organism survives. If more energy goes out than goes in, then the organism's credit score goes in the tank, and the organism will eventually die. So, all organisms seek energy input according to their life's design.

Fish are both predator and prey. That is, they are midway on the scale from total prey (a gnu) to total predator (a lion). Fish eat other organisms, and in turn get eaten by yet other organisms. Thus, fish are constantly watching for food, but always with an eye out for possible predators. Their food is basically anything smaller than themselves.

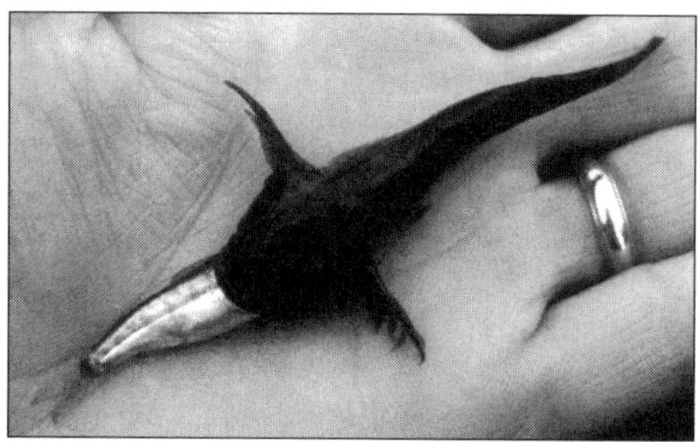

This sculpin died trying to ingest a fish nearly its own size.

Since we know that fish are predators, then if we can find their prey, we can usually find the fish. Reading waters can be about finding fish indirectly by finding their food. That was the point of the first two stories in Chapter One. Reading waters can be about finding the places where the food lives and then looking for feeding fish in such places. That's the point of the third through the sixth stories in Chapter One. Reading waters involves knowing how fish feed and taking advantage of that understanding. That's also the point of the third through seventh stories in Chapter One. Reading waters is also about selecting the best method for getting our imitation to the fish so that the fake seems real.

Knowing what fish eat and how they eat it is also a key ingredient to reading waters. As an example, when Ed Rice and I were fishing for payara, we also had opportunities to fish for peacock bass. They are totally different critters. Payara are open-water fish that hunt their prey in active pursuit. Their mouths are designed to scissor their prey into pieces in a single vicious bite. Peacock bass are heavy cover dwellers, ambushing their prey and vacuuming it down in one instantaneous gulp. To fish for payara in the places where peacock bass live would be totally unproductive. To look for peacock bass in the heavy currents where the roving payara hang out would likewise be totally unproductive.

Equally unproductive would be fishing for payara or tiger fish with insect imitations. They simply don't eat insects. If insects were a foot or two long and weighed a half-pound or more, maybe they would be interested, but offering them a mayfly dun imitation would otherwise be futile. When we went for payara and tigers, we took flies to imitate baitfish. When I was using the four-foot rod on the Bighorn, I used an insect imitation because that's what the trout were eating. So, knowing what fish eat helps when reading waters because it guides us to the places where the right food is found.

People like to fish for trout because they are found worldwide in lakes, streams, and the sea, and because they eat such a large variety of food items. One can pursue trout exclusively on the dry fly, go after them with nymphs, pitch huge baitfish and leech imitations, or happily blend it all and play the conditions at hand. No matter which approach you choose, reading waters will be essential to success.

Life Rule #3: Reproduce!

And of course, there's Life Rule Number Three: "Reproduce!" Generally in fish, and especially in sport fish, reproduction is a once-a-year event. Game and fish regulations may prevent anglers from fishing during such periods as a way to protect the congregated fish. But, then again, it may be the only time that some fish are readily available to the sport fisher. For instance, catching king salmon in the open ocean with a fly rod is not readily done, so anglers are permitted to fish for them when they move into the steams to reproduce. Fishing during reproductive times must be carefully controlled to assure that there are enough fish to reproduce so that the following generation is not diminished. Unfortunately that is not always the case with commercial harvesting. Sport fishers need to take a keen interest in all harvest methods, and promote laws that assure protection for the continued propagation of a sustainable population of all fish.

A river full of sockeye salmon working to satisfy Life Rule #3.

Fishing for spawning fish is often the time when fly fishers have the best chance to catch the biggest fish of the year. The fish are concentrated, and finding the big boys may entail no more than looking for them. In the Lake States, for example, the fall runs of salmon are followed by a run of huge browns. These fish are normally out in very deep lake waters and inaccessible to the fly fisher. But when they move in to spawn, they're mighty easy to spot, even in water several feet deep. My biggest, to-date brown is an 19-pound male that vacuumed a size 2, black stonefly nymph right off the bottom. It was a fish that had moved up from Lake Michigan with a group of other browns. It's rather easy to tell a brown of that size from the smaller ones in the group!

But it isn't always about catching the spawning fish. There are steelhead that follow the fall-running salmon, too. The steelhead don't spawn until spring, but they certainly eat salmon eggs in the fall. This may be a key to their winter survival in the streams. Obviously, finding the steelhead means looking behind pairs of spawning salmon. And the fly? Usually a single egg. After all, if the "hatch" is eggs, then matching the hatch means using an egg imitation. But I've have steelhead nail a big black leech that I was swinging for salmon, too. Or grab a stonefly nymph that I was bouncing down to a big

A mouse fly will pull very large fish to the surface to feed.

brown. It's a terrible thing when one gets upset that a 30-inch steelhead took the fly instead of the 34-inch brown that one was fishing to!

In Alaska, the rainbow fishing is almost exclusively for fish that are eating salmon chow. From mid-June right through to ice-up, there are salmon and salmon parts in all the streams, and the trout know how to take advantage of the abundant food. Only early in the year are the trout really susceptible to dry flies, nymphs, and small wet flies. Sure, one can find the occasional 'bow that will take a mayfly imitation or small nymph when the salmon are in, but they are few and far between. Up the ante and toss a huge mouse imitation out there, though, and the story may have a different ending.

And since we're talking about reading waters to help find chow and feeding fish, let's read the bank, too. Mice are found in areas with lots of grass and brush, so when fishing waters where these are prevalent, it behooves the angler to look for holding waters where a mouse fly could be explosively effective. One year, when fishing the Talachulitna River in Alaska, I tied on a big, tan Strip Leech and began fishing down a long corner pool. At first, nothing. Then I drove the big fly hard, and plopped it down tight against the far bank, where grasses, brush and fallen timber served as decoration. The fly moved about a foot, and I had a very nice rainbow. This was repeated on nearly every cast that I could get right to the other bank. Several fish into the excitement, a rainbow heaved up a northern water shrew, and the light bulb went on. They were taking the leech as a diving shrew. From then on, every place that I could reach across with a cast, I pounded that tan leech to great effect. Reading waters isn't always about reading waters; it may be about reading the land forms and vegtetation around the water.

Currents and Their Tongues

A stream can be defined as a body of water moving down-slope in a channel. Carefully notice the following: (1) **It is a body of water**, (2) **it is moving**, (3) **it moves down-slope**, and (4) **it is in a channel**. Gravity pulls the water down-slope, and the greater the slope the greater the force that the moving body of water has. Since it is moving in a channel, the force is directed along the path of the channel. The movement of material along a directed pathway is called a current. Thus, we can say that a stream is a current of water moving in a channel *(Figure 2.1)*. Anything in the channel that is not

Figure 2.1. *A stream is a current of water flowing in a channel..*

somehow affixed to the channel will be swept down-current.

Thus, we can make a blanket statement about all living organisms in a stream: Somehow, they have to negate the effects of the currents or be swept away. Plants do it by roots that anchor them in the bottom. Single-celled algae do it by attaching themselves to rocks or other bottom structures. In-stream rocks are slippery because of their algae coating—called *periphyton* (peri = around; phyta = plants). Insects negate the effects of the currents by living under the rocks, in the cracks between them, burrowing in the bottom, flattening themselves tightly against bottom structures, living in leaf pack and inside logs and sticks, and cementing themselves to bottom structures. Fish just stay out of fast currents unless moving from place to place; even then they will follow the thread of least resistance as they swim in the current.

In moving water, fish generally hold in one position and allow the currents to bring them their food. This is not because they're decadent and lazy, but rather because it is the most energy efficient way to hunt and gather. Remember, *Energy in minus Energy out = live or die*. Now, here we need to distinguish between the term, "current," which denotes the general, overall movement of water downslope in a channel, and areas within the stream where the currents may be tightly concentrated. These areas, called "current tongues," are also concentrators of food items *(Figure 2.2)*. For example, at

Figure 2.2. *Current tongues are visible between the boulders.*

the edges of a midstream boulder are two current tongues, one along either side. Because current tongues concentrate food, they also concentrate fish. Current tongues are a major feature in reading waters, and we need to pay attention to them wherever we find them.

Fish Lies

The place that the fish holds in the currents is called its "lie." Some people call this place a "holding lie," but really, all lies are "holding" in the sense that they are the places that fish remain positioned, facing into the current. We can identify **three broad categories** of lies: **sheltering lies**, **feeding lies**, and **prime lies**. Each category is based upon what it provides to the fish. All three lies are important to the fish at various times during the day Understanding how fish interact with such places can be critically important to the angler's success, or lack thereof. Discerning why fish are where fish are is one of the primary goals of reading waters, and thus learning the features of each lie is of paramount importance.

Protection from Currents

In streams, there is one rule that applies to every lie: *All lies must provide protection from currents.* Places that do not provide protection from the force of the moving water will simply not be lies.

"Wait a minute," you might be saying, "I've caught many trout out of swiftly moving water." Me, too. But just because they were in a stretch of fast water does not mean they were holding *in* the fast water. They were lying in a place of calm within the zone of moving water. Fish cannot swim endlessly. No animal can run, or even walk, endlessly. It's back to the conservation of energy.

Like some cars, fish sport a pin strip down the length of their bodies. It's the lateral line—lateral meaning "side"*(Figure 2.3)*. It may be distinctly darker than the side of the fish or it may only be seen as a raised area along the side. The lateral line consists of a series of interconnected "U" shaped tubes filled with a jelly like material. The open end of each "U"" is facing to the exterior of the body. The lateral line extends forward around the fish's eyes and onto its lips, although in these areas the structure is much more difficult to discern with the naked eye. Nerve endings line the bottoms of the tubes. Waves in the water generated by displacement (a minnow swimming, an angler wading, currents, and so on) create pressure on the material in the lateral line. The pressure of this displacement is sensed by the nerves. The lateral line not only allows the fish to detect prey and predators, but also allows the fish to align itself most advantageously in the currents, to space itself in a school of fish, and to swim with the synchrony of the school. Studies have shown that the lateral line can detect differences in currents between the two sides of the fish's body as small as 1/25 of an inch per second.

With the help of its lateral line, a fish can easily find the places where the currents will allow it to park without having to work. Fish rely on the lateral line to help them find that just-right spot to stay out of the currents while looking for food or hiding from a predator.

Speaking of which, trudging along the stream bank like an elephant in a conga line is not smart. The pounding vibrations of one's feet transfer into the water, and fish can pick up on one's presence in a hurry. They either flee or they zip up their lips and sink to the bottom. Walk like a stealthy heron, and stay hidden. Always assume that the fish can both see and hear you. And wade quietly, too; fish know you're in the water, big fish *always* know." If they can "hear" you hiking on shore, they can certainly "hear" you waltzing around in their living rooms.

Reading waters is not always about reading waters.

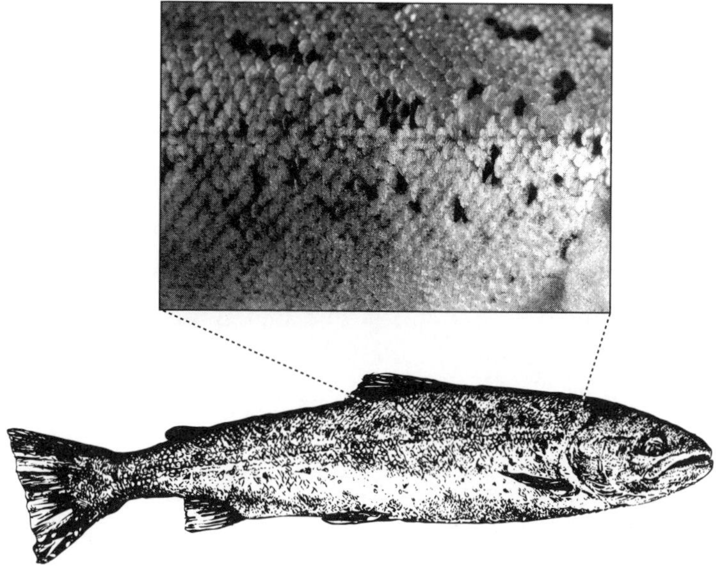

Figure 2.3. *"The better to sense you, my dear." The lateral line on this salmon is readily visible.*

Sheltering Lie

A sheltering lie is a place fish go to get protection from predators. Fish do not go there to eat. It's a place where fish go, zip their mouths shut, and hunker down until they feel it's safe to venture out again. Generally speaking, a sheltering lie is under something: under the bank, under a rock or log, under deep water, under vegetation, and so on. And as Jason likes to say, when it comes to saltwater, the sheltering lie may simply be, "Away—as fast as possible!" If we're talking the flats, that "away" may mean the nearest deeper water. If we're talking deeper water already, that "away" may mean straight down, or into bottom structure. I hooked a grouper one time that made some rather amazing, fly-line destroying use of bottom structure!

My old friend, Royce Dam, fishing in the Yellowstone backcountry and standing knee deep in sheltering lies. Every fish he hooked ran into the weeds.

How long any given fish spends in a sheltering lie depends on the fish itself. I once caught a very nice brown in a small spring creek in Montana during a heavy PMD hatch. I came back to the same spot several hours later while the hatch was still on, and not a single fish was rising, or even visible in that spot. When I caught the brown, the area had been full of feeding fish, which all fled for cover when they heard the thrashing sound of that big trout. But conversely, there's the female salmon that I described in *Fishing the Film* that took the fly six times in a row, and escaped all six times.

Another time, during a fall fishing excursion for big browns, I spotted a nice fish holding at the top of a small current break. It was in the shadows, and hard to see clearly. On my second cast, the fly snagged it in the tail, and it thrashed and ran off downstream like a raging bull. I broke it off immediately, but feared it was long gone. By the time I had tied on another fly, the fish was back and acting aggressive. On the second cast it grabbed the fly with serious determination. It was a 30-inch male with a monster kype. And yes, I did get my other fly back. That fish was an exception, though. By and large one can say that fish which are spooked quit feeding—at least for a while.

Mostly, when fish quit feeding, they head off to a sheltering lie. A major part of reading waters is watching constantly for sheltering lies. First, fish in sheltering lies are not feeding; so don't bother casting there. Second, and far more important, is the fact that when fish are hooked, they spook and head *right now* for the nearest sheltering lie. This is not about finding fish at all; it's about fighting them. If one knows that a fish is headed for a hiding hole the second it's spooked (read, hooked) then one can anticipate the fish's movements by knowing where the sheltering lies are. Suddenly the angler is in control, not the fish.

Most anglers fight fish by what I call the prayer method. They hook a good fish, lift the rod straight up, clasp their hands together, and pray, "Please, God, let me land this fish." And then, no matter how much coaching God actually gives them, they continue to hold the rod straight up, as if invoking some sort of mystery incantation. Here's the bottom line: If you know where the sheltering lies are, you can take the fight to the fish, and more times than not, win. As we explore the various features of stream structure in subsequent chapters, I will point out a variety of sheltering lies.

The Feeding Lie

A feeding lie is a place a fish goes to eat. Now remember, all lies must provide protection from currents; so it is with the feeding lie. At the same time, there needs to be some sort of current that will bring the fish sufficient food in order to make it worth the time to sit in the lie and wait. So, often one will find fish parked at the very edge of a current tongue, especially where it concentrates food. On Henry's Fork of the Snake, in the famous Harriman Ranch section, there are many feeding lies right in close to shore where a rock, a clump of sod, a bush, or other structure pushes out a short ways into the currents. The narrow current tongues set up on the stream side of these objects concentrates the food, and the slow currents behind the obstruction makes a perfect place for a fish to park. They're either right on the very inside edge of the current tongue or actually downstream from the obstruction several feet and right in the current tongue where it starts to diffuse.

Sneaking up on a big New Zealand brown trout (arrow) that is holding in a feeding lie along the shallow currents at the edge of a strong riffle. This is the fish shown (after a successful cast) on the first page of Chapter One.

These spots are in shallow water, and offer no protection. Therefore, the fish feeding in them tend to be very spooky, and as such require greater caution in wading and casting. And where do those fish go when hooked? On the Fork they head for the deep water and weed beds in the center of the river. In *Fishing the Film*, there's a story of a big bow that I hooked in just such a place, using a Down-and-Across Dead Drift approach. It raced out so fast that just the pressure of the water against the 6X tippet broke it.

Another time, Jason and I were fishing on Henry's Fork, and found a pod of nice fish in tight against the bank and feeding subsurface. We were hunkered down behind some tall grasses and casting only a few feet to them. A big boy nabbed my tiny midge larva and jumped straight up. We both estimated the fish at about six pounds. I ran up the hill behind me in an attempt to get the line as high as possible, but the fish was in the middle of the river and the middle of the weeds before I could sprint the few yards up the bank. I felt the 5X tippet rubbing and catching, and then the fish was gone.

"Why didn't you jump in and run after it?" Jason asked.

"I didn't want to spook the other fish," I explained.

"Well, if we get another, in we go," Jason replied.

In a few minutes I was in the batter's box again, and I connected to a very healthy, but slightly smaller rainbow. This time I did jump in, wading as fast as I could after the fish. It was in the weeds like a lightning bolt, but I was over it in a couple of seconds and worked the leader free. We played the weed dance at least a half dozen more times before I got the fish into open water where I could keep it from the weeds. The 'bow was quite tired by that time. Keeping it where I wanted was easy. My net slid neatly under the trout, and there was the little size 22 midge larva, tucked neatly into the corner of the fish's mouth. Sometimes reading waters is not just about reading waters.

The big 'bow and I had a bit of a dance through the weedy sheltering lies.

As noted, feeding lies are usually in shallow water (or sometimes in deeper water, but with the fish holding in a shallow position. There are a couple of reasons for this. First, if the fish is watching the surface, then it doesn't want to hold in fast mid-column waters and try to feed on surface items. Second, it doesn't want to swim up through any more water than is absolutely necessary to catch its food—the old energy conservation thing, yet again. Third, if it's too deep, it can't see surface items well. Fish feeding on subsurface items—like the fish we found on the Fork—may hold in shallow water because shallow water is an excellent place to find food (most of the food organisms live in shallower waters), and because the water column is, to say it the best way, shallow. There's not as much water to watch from top to bottom, and it's therefore easier to see the food items, and to get to them. Then, too, any lie that has the necessary ingredients to make it a good place to watch the surface also has the ingredients for watching the subsurface currents, as well.

Now, notice something: The water is usually *shallow*. There are lots of shallow water places in streams, many of which anglers tend to view as "wade-through" territory. *Fishing is not a wading contest!* One of the common threads running though this series of books is the angler as predator; in fact, one of the books in this series is entitled, *The Angler as Predator*. Everything that we do as fly fishers hinges directly or indirectly on this simple premise. When we, as fly fishers, finally view ourselves as honest-to-goodness predators, and begin acting as such, suddenly this catching fish thing is not nearly so hard. It often demands a change in our attitudes and behaviors, but then, learning the correct way to participate in any sport or game requires learning the basic precepts and applying them well.

As I often say: "Don't wade it until you fish it" (within reason, of course). This was a lesson I learned early in life. I was stumbling along the rocky edge of a riffle early one morning, as only one can stumble in oversized hip boots ("You'll grow into them"), when suddenly, right there in front of me, one more stumbling step away, was a very large brown. As my youthful memory plays it back, it was certainly one of the 27-inch behemoths than someone pulled out of that river every year, but more likely it was 18 to 20 inches. To a boy who only caught such fish in dreams, it was, none-the-less, a "monster." It saw me just as I saw it, and there was a thrashing and tearing of water that was a sight to behold. The fish bolted out of there, too.

What the heck was it doing there? I saw the fresh husks of stoneflies and *Isonychia* mayfly nymphs on the rocks at the water's edge, and understood. It was there eating. I cannot begin to tell you how many times I looked in that spot again over the years and never saw another fish. But I did find others in shallows all along the river. Never the "monster" of that day, but plenty of smaller ones to keep me occupied. Again, as we look at river features in upcoming chapters, we'll explore a whole series of feeding lies.

The Prime Lie

Now comes the crème de la crème, the really good spot, the prime lie. This is a combination of the other two. That is, it's **both a sheltering lie and a feeding lie rolled into one.** However, it can have attributes that a strictly feeding lie does not have. First, since it has the features of a sheltering lie, it's under something—under a bank, under a log, under a rock, under deep water, under a foam patch, under fast water, and so on. And like a feeding lie, there has to be a food source of relative concentration. But unlike a feeding lie, there is no restriction on water depth. Prime lies can be in relatively shallow water or in deep water. The only restrictions are: (1) cover, (2) food.

Jason is fishing the prime lie at the head of a pool in the cover shot. Notice all the current tongues, too.

There are many such places, and knowing what to look for and how to approach them and fish them is one of the prime skills of reading waters. And of course, we will discuss these in detail throughout the succeeding chapters. But I want to make this note right now, to keep the "little gray cells" going. If a prime lie has the attributes of a sheltering lie and you hook a fish in a feeding lie, it will go to a prime lie just as fast as it will go to a sheltering lie. Therefore, we note both sheltering lies and prime lies as refuge sites, and plot our fish fighting strategies accordingly.

The Passage of Seasons

In many streams, most notably freestoners, sheltering lies, feeding lies, and prime lies may or may not be sheltering lies, feeding lies, and prime lies, depending upon the season. As the rivers wax and wane over the course of the year, sometimes quite dramatically, new lies are established or old ones are dried up. Anglers of the spring usually find the highest waters of the year, and consequently find a different set of lies than those fishing the lower waters of summer. An angler fishing the river in spring, and then returning later in the year to fish the same places will often not recognize any of the lies located during the earlier trip. Rapids have become riffles, pools have become flats, shorelines that were tight to the trees now show lots of gravel, and so on.

In the spring and summer of 1986, Jason and I videotaped *Bow River Adventure* in southern Alberta. When we arrived in Calgary in June, the guys at the fly shop informed us that we'd managed to hit runoff right on dead center. To assist with water levels being as high as possible, rain had been falling for two weeks. The river, which normally runs around 3,300 cfs was charging head-long at well over 9,000 cfs. We rigged up sink tips and big, black leeches and sped off on what would normally be a full-day's float. Our ride instead finished up around noon. But what a ride, and what a day's fishing! We just read the river as if it were in normal flow. The banks were lined with small willows, a variety of bushes, wild roses, and big cottonwoods. At the first patch of small willows, I heaved the big leech into a narrow slot in the patch and stripped it out. The willows literally shook as a big brown charged out through them to inhale the fly. And so it went throughout the drift. We pulled fish out of rose bushes, from behind the cottonwoods, in the lee of brush clumps, and so on. Jason topped the day with an enormous brown that was holding in a confluence line behind a temporary island created where the floodwater surged out of croplands.

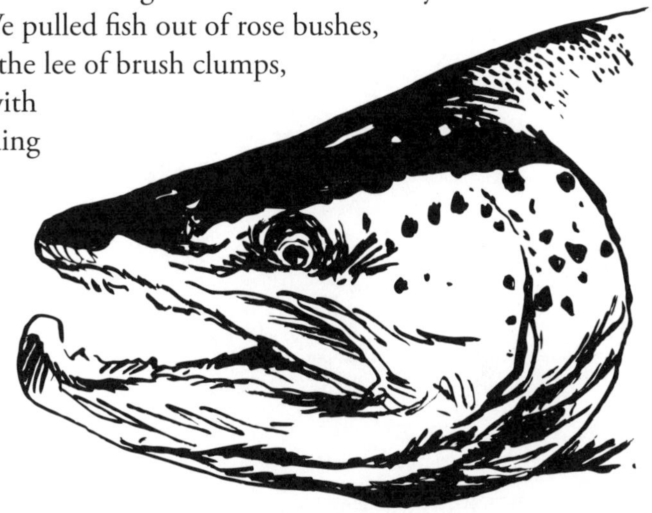

We returned later in the season (grasshopper time) to videotape another mood of the Bow. It was a gentle giant. Weed beds waved to us from the crystalline currents, mayflies were on the wing, and hoppers were everywhere. The banks that had been underwater earlier in the year were now four to five feet above the water's surface. We couldn't even find many of the places where we'd caught fish in the early season because there was no longer any water in them. But a whole host of new places had opened up, and reading waters allowed us to find fish every day to fulfill the camera's appetite.

Always be ready to read waters anew, even when returning to the same place on the same stream only a few days apart. Hatch conditions, temperature conditions, and so on can put the fish in different places from day to day. My wife, Nancy, and I were fishing the Madison one year over a period of a couple of weeks. During our time there, the PMDs started hatching. Knowing that the nymphs would be active a couple of hours before the hatch, we drove to a favorite stretch of water and began nymphing. Places that had offered nary a fish the week before were suddenly hot-spots. The entire stretch of river had to be re-scrutinized for potential feeding lies, but it was certainly worth the effort required.

With this idea of water-level change in mind, think about tailwaters, especially tailwaters that are at the mercy of significant generation schedules. In essence, such tailwaters exhibit a daily cycle of "tides." When the generators are on, it's definitely "high tide." When they're off, it's "low tide," and sometimes, *really* low tide. In addition to the alteration of the three lies and other aspects of reading water, fishing such places can be dangerous if one gets trapped in mid-stream by a sudden release of water. Always, always (did I mention always?) check with the appropriate agency about release schedules, and pay close attention to them!

A tailwater at "low tide." When the generators are on, those gravel bars are under several feet of rushing water. This makes for two totally different "reads."

Just Right Porridge

A classic spring creek with stable banks and uniform, cool flows.

The passage of seasons not only changes water levels, it changes water temperatures as well. Obviously, the water is warmer in summer and colder in the winter, but that variation may be large or small. In some tailwaters, like New Mexico's San Juan, the water temperatures in the summer are only a few degrees warmer than in winter.

Natural spring creeks vary little in temperature from summer to winter, especially right at their source. Obviously, the further downstream from the source that one gets, the more the creek is subject to change with the air temperature. Even so, spring creeks change less in temperature from summer to winter than do freestone streams. Thus, it is possible to fish streams like the famed Armstrong Spring Creek, Nelson's Spring Creek, DePuy's Spring Creek, and others, every month of the year—without having to resort to ice fishing in the winter.

Freestone streams run the classic warm/cold cycle that is intimately linked to the changing of seasons. In winter, ice can sometimes cover them fully. In summer they are warm enough for people to swim in. This wildly swinging temperature regime can put serious pressure on the fish, especially in the depths of winter and in the height of summer. Winter conditions can create anchor ice and drifting ice crystals that can cause serious damage to the fish population. But it is the summer temperatures that so strongly affect the fly fisher's ability to find feeding fish.

When the stream temperatures get into the mid-70s F (mid-20s C), trout begin to feel stressed and may not feed until the water temperatures drop. In streams that do hold trout year-round, but in which summer, day-time water temperatures reach the mid to high 70s F, the best fishing is often right at dawn after the water has cooled all night. Then too, fish may move out of the warmer stream into cooler tributaries or move to areas in the stream where there are spring seeps on the bottom, and so on. In lakes and in the ocean, fish will move to find their ideal temperature and oxygen levels.

A classic freestoner in New Zealand. The water is highly subject to flooding and the banks are largely devoid of vegetation.

One can read the waters until the cows come home, but if the fish are not there, you're going to end up leafing through nothing but empty pages. Know the preferred temperature ranges for the species that you intend to fish for, and then hunt them with a thermometer when conditions are less than ideal. More on these requirements in our upcoming book, *The Angler as Predator*.

Stream Physiognomy

Physiognomy is just a fancy way to say that streams have a specific shape for a reason. Water running down hill and carving a channel flows straighter the steeper the slope. Conversely, the less the slope, the more the stream meanders back and forth. Streams in very flat areas tend to really loop around. They can literally loop back on themselves and eventually cut off corners to form oxbow lakes.

Yellowstone Park's Firehole, with its hot springs and geysers, has been called "the strangest trout stream on Earth," but it still meanders true to the form of most streams.

In the classic trout stream, the water usually digs deeply in the corners and dumps the load on the straight-aways between corners, forming riffles, and thereby creating the classic riffle-pool configuration. And while this is the paradigm of river physiognomy, there are many exceptions. Thus it is that streams and rivers present a host of possible configurations that the fly fisher can explore. We will examine many of these in the course of this text, but never say never. There is absolute certainty that you will find exceptions to the examples that I've used here. Always be ready to use your knowledge of the way fish interact with currents, cover, and food sources when reading waters, regardless of their "physiognomy."

Fish Numbers

Not unexpectedly, but perhaps often overlooked, is the effect of the overall size of the fish population on their distribution in any stream, lake, or ocean flat. The greater the number of fish in any one body of water, the more they will fill all the available lies.

Some large, highly prolific rivers may hold as many as 10,000 to 20,000 trout per mile. With such densities, the super prime lie at the top of a pool can seem almost black with fish, and every good feeding lie will hold several trout during a heavy hatch. But then, I've fished rivers where the trout population was only a few hundred per mile. In such waters, only the very best of the best lies will hold fish, and unless the angler really keys in on these spots, the fishing can be a bit thin, indeed.

I've seen the effects of fish numbers on distribution during summer trips to Alaska and during the fall runs of salmon and trout into the tributaries of the Great Lakes. Obviously before the run, one can fish themselves silly, and not find a single fish in the best of the best lies. When the run starts, the first fish grab the best spots. As the run peaks, every spot, even those that are marginally acceptable, are filled with fish.

I've seen the same thing on the flats. One day every possible spot is occupied by feeding fish. The next day, the only thing the high tide brings in is water.

I've also hunted cruisers along a lake shore when they were as thick as the proverbial fleas on a dog's back and took any fly you offered, only to return the next day and find them thinner than hen's teeth and as spooky as deer.

Fish Follow Food

Fish do not stay in one place continually and wait for food. How silly would it be for a deer to hang out in one edge of a freshly plowed field and wait for the grass to grow? All living organisms, and that includes old fishermen, go in search of food if there's none readily available.

Fish move onto the flats (whether lake or ocean) to feed when the food is there. When the food disappears, the fish leave. In lakes, fish will move to varying depths very quickly in search of food (more on this in Chapter Ten).

I guess the upshot of all of this is that reading waters is not merely locating specific stream, lake, or ocean features, but rather is an integrated process that draws on all the available information that the angler has at hand. Make this your goal.

The Song of the Little Stream

Her song is thin and light, with notes that rise like wisps of wind. But there are lessons aplenty in her thin waters, lessons that linger a lifetime, and hold true across the whole of the face of fly fishing. They are lessons that I learned early. Lessons from the waters of the little stream.

Growing up in rural Pennsylvania, in the dissected Allegheny Plateau of the state's northwest corner, I had access to many little streams that paid their tribute to the bigger Sugar Creek, to the still larger French Creek, and then to the mighty Allegheny. Streams with names like Beatty Run, Foster Run, Wolf Run, Little Sandy, 16 Mile Creek, and many others. They were forest streams, by and large, interrupted on occasion by a cow pasture or hay field, usually in their lower reaches. In their hills grew all manner of spring ephemerals—wild flowers that made the bouquets for my mother. There were hints among the older men of wild ginseng, though I never found any. And it was there that my great grandmother gathered the roots and herbs for her "grandma's salve," that was liberally applied to everything from skinned knees to sunburns.

The song of the little streams in my childhood was first and foremost a song of brook trout. Brilliantly colored and wild beyond belief, they rarely exceeded eight inches in length; many were just legal, many were too tiny to make a bite for even a small boy. But they were trout, and they did all the things that wild trout do; especially dash off in a puff of fine silt at the first hint of footsteps or an errant shadow. From these little fish, I learned to hunt trout, not just go fishing.

Foster Run

Foster Run starts high in the forestlands. It is strictly small—most places one can step or easily jump across its narrow channel. In the woodlands, when I fished it, there were downfalls from seasons past. They blocked the stream and they overhung its waters. It felt wild and free in the forest, and I loved to go there to hike along the stream and find spots where I could get a fly in the water. And getting the fly in the water was the trick. In the jungle of bushes and downed trees, casting was a foreign movement.

There was no room for, nor any need of, casting. Even if there had been room for casting, it was not the most effective way to catch the brookies in such a tiny stream. Tossing a line onto that water would have spooked every fish. No, the way to fish Foster Run, high in its headwater pools and pockets, was to feed the line downstream. And, I discovered, that true to its intent, the Mickey Finn was a wonderful brook trout fly.

I would position myself upstream from a corner pool, where the waters ran back under the bank, or above a fallen log where foam piled upon foam, or perhaps, in a couple of spots, where the water had gouged out a dark pocket along the edge of an ancient boulder carried there during the last glaciation. It was essential to stay hidden, but that was the least of my worries in the forest. There were more than enough trees to go around.

I'd feed the line out into the main current. While keeping it tight enough so that the fly would hang, I'd slowly pay out line until the fly disappeared under the bank or log, or into the dark slot along the boulders. Then, holding the line so it didn't slide out any further, I'd move the rod tip back upstream and draw the fly out from the cover. When I could see the fly clearly, I'd move the rod tip back downstream and allow the fly to work back into the cover again. I'd move the line from side to side so the fly swept across the currents and back. Then, I'd pull it out of cover and let it run back in again. Most of the time I'd get a fish or two out of every likely spot. That meant any place where there was overhead cover with a current running into it: prime lies.

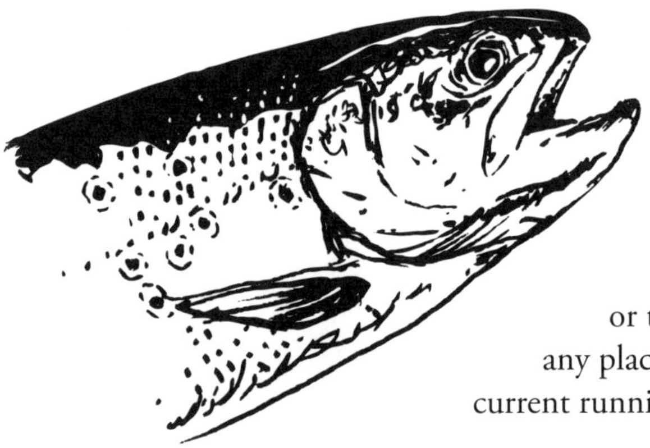

I didn't know they were lies, prime or otherwise. In those days, they were just the places that fish could hide, and it didn't take much to see such places on the micro-scale of that little stream. Things like riffles, runs, flats, and other characteristics of stream physiognomy meant nothing there; trout only held in those places with more than a few inches of depth and hidden away from the prying eyes of predators.

It was a baptism that has stayed with me. Even now, nearly 60 years later, I watch all waters, no matter how small or large for "micro-lies"—tiny spots where fish can hold, especially if they're prime lies. Trout can be in very small spots that many anglers simply walk by, never bothering to even look at or explore with a cast or two. One day I was fishing Armstrong Spring Creek during the PMD hatch. Other anglers were working the mid-stream rising rainbows to great effect, but it got old to me. Not because the 12 to 14-inch bows weren't great fun, they were, but that day I wanted some serious fish. So I changed to a 3X tippet and lashed on a big, black, Strip Leech.

Wading the middle of the stream, I cast down-and-across into every tiny spot I could locate that was up tight to the bank. Many were covered with watercress. Some were under bushes and overhanging grass. A few were under places where the sod had slumped. And still others were just a tiny sliver of dark water against the bank. They were full of browns, big ones, and my craving for large trout was well satisfied by evening. Every fish ate that fly like it was its last meal. Several times, I plopped the big leech right in front of a cress bed, and before the fly had drifted six inches, a big head came out and ate it.

The big browns on Armstrong Spring Creek held under small bits of bank-side cover, seemingly too tiny at times, to hold them.

Now that I know where those big fish hold, I go there and try to find them eating emergers or dries during a hatch. It can be challenging fishing. Don't think that these "micro-lies" are just small stream or spring creek phenomena, though. They're present on all streams, and are usually overlooked. Spend time watching every potential spot, micro or macro.

Now, back to Foster Run. It broke out of the forest lands at the top of the Bean's family farm and ran through the cattle pasture. The Bean family was quite kind and generous to us kids. We could fish there anytime we wanted to without asking, they told us, only make certain that closed gates were kept closed and open gates were left open; and by the way, stay out of the pasture when the bull was in there. No one that I know of ever broke their rules. One doesn't mess with bulls, and living in farm country, everyone knew the rule of gates.

But whenever the cows were in the barn, we'd fish the pasture. The stream was bigger by the time it got to the open lands—one had to get a running start to jump across it—and its banks held beds of watercress. The plant's peppery bite was always a refreshing crunch on a hot summer day. In this stretch of the stream, it was the undercut sod banks and cress beds that held the fish. On rare occasion we'd even spook a fish that was out in the open water watching for hoppers or other terrestrials. Out technique didn't change, only the places that we'd explore with the downstream approach. We never fished dries; we never saw anything rise, and so the idea never crossed our minds.

Occasionally, or perhaps I should say rarely, we'd get a fish in the 10-inch range; that's what kept us coming back. In the heat of a summer day, on the Snyder farm, just downstream from the Bean's place, I'd build sod dams with my pal, Butch, to make a "swimming hole," although they were really not much more than wallows. In the process, we'd hunt for snapping turtles. We'd explore back under the overhanging sod banks until we'd find one, and then feel along the top of its shell to find the ridges. They point rearward, so we'd work back to the tail, grab it, and haul the turtle out. It was while doing this that we also flushed trout out from under the banks. We'd remember where we'd seen them and come back in the cool of the evening or in the morning mist and try to catch them, still using the same downstream approach.

Beatty Run

Beatty Run was closer than Foster Run, and it was bigger, at least near its terminus. Still a little stream overall, it had to be waded to cross it, no jump could ever clear it.

A bank-side log with its attendant foam patch was always a great place to find a recently stocked rainbow or hold-over brown on Beatty Run.

It also had riffles, runs, straight pools, corner pools, log jams, boulders, and undercuts galore. It was a place that my older brother, Val, and I could easily walk to and fish. We started with worms, using our one-piece steel rods, bait casting reels, and black nylon line. Later, it was a place that I explored with flies.

Still not a hospitable place for the caster, except where it ran through a neighbor's pasture, it did, none-the-less, hold trout in the open waters of its deeper riffles and runs. These were deep enough to be prime lies, too, and I'd pound them mercilessly once I knew where the fish were most likely to be. I fished flies with the same downstream technique as on Foster Run, and it still worked. I mostly caught brookies, but once in a while, I'd get a rainbow or brown that had come up from Sugar Creek. That was the bonus that kept me fishing Beatty's waters.

And of course the nearer one got to the confluence of Beatty Run and Sugar Creek, the greater the chance that I'd get a 'bow or brown. The last section ran along the end of Sleepy Hollow Golf Course, through a strip of forestland where we kids often hunted golf balls to sell. This last section was filled with undercuts, pockets, pools, and riffles. Reading waters here was more like it was in Sugar Creek itself. But again, it was the prime lies that I worked over, hoping that a recently stocked rainbow had wandered into the creek, or that maybe a holdover brown had secreted itself in a dark hole.

Wolf Creek

It was in Wolf Creek that I discovered the real importance of undercut-bank prime lies. If a current runs back under a bank, then that place will be a prime lie if the water is at least deep enough to cover the fish. A friend and I had been exploring a new section that we'd never fished, when we came upon a corner pool that was perhaps three feet deep and only six feet wide. The current sliced deeply into the root structure of the trees and brush along the high bank, forming an overhanging web of soil, roots, and grass that draped some four feet from its top, down to its contact with the water. As we came up on the pool, a big shadow slipped back under the bank. We'd never seen a trout that large in this or any of the other small streams that we fished. I waded in very quietly and looked into the undercut from upstream. There, calmly parked about 15 feet away, was a 20–inch brown.

A 20-inch Wolf Creek brown taught me about undercuts and gave me years worth of youthful bragging rights.

I didn't figure that the fish would take my fly, but, I wasn't going to pass up the chance. So I poked the rod into the undercut, dropped the fly in the water and fed line down to the brown. The fly hung out near its face, but got zero response. I kept it swimming around for a while, because I just couldn't give up on the biggest trout I'd ever seen in one of our favorite small waters. Then, as if possessed, the brown grabbed the fly and went nuts. It didn't rush away, however. It must have been in its hiding hole and wasn't about to leave. I finally wrestled it out, more by brute force and sheer serendipity than by any craft or skill. It was the biggest brown—heck, it was the biggest trout—that I had ever caught, and it gave me bragging rights for years to come.

Little Sandy

When the most prized of all youthful milestones finally fell into my possession, the angling world opened like never before: I had my driver's license! My father was a roofing contractor, and always had several pickups around. He gave in to my need to fish, and often loaned me a truck, or would drop me and a friend at an out-of-town stream near where he was working for the day, picking us up on the way home.

But it was the days when I got a truck to drive that my friend, John Grove, and I would head out to Little Sandy Creek for a full day's fishing expedition. We often got there with the sunrise and didn't get home until after dark. And we definitely caught fish. A short stretch of Little Sandy had very recently been made fly-fishing only, and we knew every rock in that stretch. We fished dries, nymphs, streamers, terrestrials, and a whole bunch of "experimental" flies. It was a wonderful world for two, mid-teen boys so hung up on, of all things, fly fishing.

The fly-only section of the Little Sandy was perhaps 30 feet wide in the widest spots, so I wouldn't classify it as small water. Upstream, though, was definitely another story. Several miles above the fly-fishing-only stretch, the stream was no bigger than Foster Run, the headwaters of Beatty Run, Wolf Creek, and other similar haunts. So, when we wanted fish to eat, we'd head up high and catch brookies. And the technique? Why, down with the Mickey Finn and other such patterns, plying the prime lies that never seemed to tire of giving up a few fish for the evening's dinner.

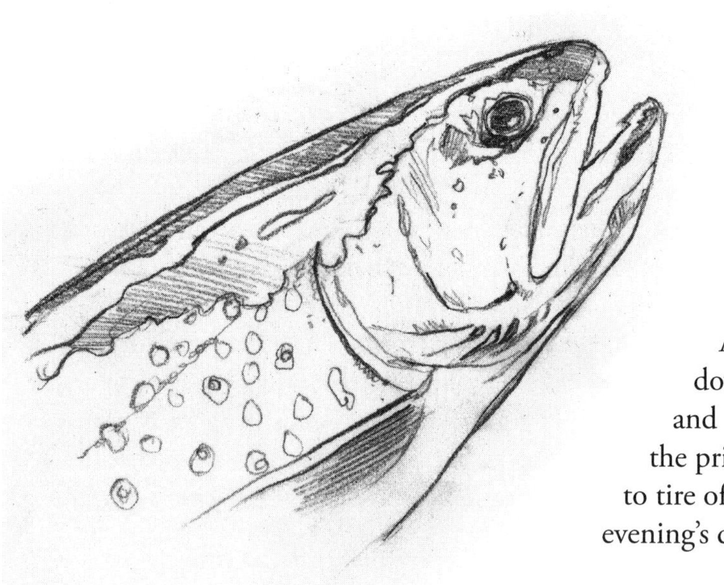

In addition to the undercuts, one of my favorite prime lies in the little stream was where a log lay across, or partly across the stream, and the currents surged directly against it (see that photo under the Beatty Run heading). The plow of the currents, pressing under the log, would dig out a scour pool beneath the log, and foam would pile up on the log face and out onto the currents for a foot or two ahead of the fallen tree. The fish would hold under the foam, usually on the bottom and just at the upper lip of the hole the currents had dug. Such a place is a superb prime lie, regardless of the stream size, as we shall see during our exploration of other streams.

Shell Creek

As a graduation present from high school, my parents sent me by train to visit my great friends, Rev. Ralph McConahy, and his wife Betty, who were pastoring a small church in Greybull, Wyoming. Ralph understood my fly fishing addiction, and had made plans for us to fish Shell Creek. It was at the upper limits of what might be considered a small stream, averaging fifteen to twenty feet wide in the stretch that we fished. It was also a mountain stream, ripping through the forest before diving head long in a series of falls and cascades into the depths of Shell Creek Canyon.

Shell Creek contained brookies, cutthroats, and rainbows that were hot for the fly, and as swift as a falcon. They would dash out of cover and grab a streamer, then rip off into the currents like lightning. It was fun to say the least. In addition to the prime lies under logs and overhanging banks, I discovered the hydraulic cushion at the front of big boulders. There were plenty of them. If the water was more than knee deep, there was sure to be fish there, watching. Again, it was the small-water, down-with-a-streamer tactic that worked so well because the swift water prevented any other approach. But by fishing down, one could guide the fly into any spot and hang it there or sweep it back and forth, or pull it up and let it drift back, etc. Fishing into the hydraulic cushion with a straight down or down-and-across approach has been a favorite ever since. I've taken many fish in this way in a variety of waters from little brooks to brawling streams and mighty rivers.

It was also on that trip that I discovered the culvert-pool prime lie. The stream shot through a culvert under the highway and dumped into a swirling pool that it had gouged out over the years. Its waters were dark with depth, with a rotating eddy at either side, where foam scurried around and around with no place to go. The fish were sometimes in the eddies, although they were a bit too shallow to be considered prime—but definitely they were feeding lies. But the dark slot that the plunging water had dug held fish at the ready, no matter what the hour. I had fished it several times before I tried throwing the Light Edson Tiger directly into the plunge. It shot deep and then jerked to a stop. At the hook set, the fish burrowed along the bottom and plowed down stream with real determination. Enough determination to snap the tippet with ease, and to leave me shaking.

I fished that spot every time we had the opportunity of go there, but I never hooked the big fish again. However, that episode would play into another discovery years later on Little Sandy Creek. But that's a story for another chapter.

Little Antietam Creek & Falling Spring Creek

My first year of college was spent at the Mont Alto Campus of Penn State University. Little Antietam Creek bounded its west side, and we could hear it gurgling past Emmanuel Chapel during Sunday morning services. It was very similar in size to Beatty Run, and it held the occasional brookie that kept things interesting. A classic freestoner, it started on the north slope of South Mountain, near where General Lee had staged his troops before retreating south to Sharpsburg, Maryland, during the Civil War.

Like most little streams it was overgrown with trees and brush, and largely neglected by everyone. The detritus of society could be found along its lower reaches that ran close to the highway, with everything from toilet seats to old tires, bottles, and cans. It's unfortunate that humans don't recognize the symptoms of the self-fouled nest until it's often too late. Although I had never fished this stream before, it had all the familiar hiding places of other streams I knew from early childhood. It was the same, only in a different place, and I could work its waters just fine.

Then, there was Falling Spring Creek. In its upper end above the local dairy, it was indeed a little stream. But little in a different way. This was in the years before the housing developments and the cascade of stream-choking gravel, sand, and silt that they created. Water cress and other rooted aquatics pressed in from either side holding the open water to a channel that only showed a few feet wide, but was in places as deep as its width. I first fished there on the opener, April 15, 1963. Of course we all got there before dawn, and fished with wet flies and streamers, catching the occasional small fish.

As the sun came up, I noticed flashes of red against the vegetation on the opposite shore of the riffle that I was fishing. I just assumed they were red horse suckers and kept fishing. But when the sun got a bit higher, I realized they were brook trout, and really nice ones. I cast myself silly and didn't hook a single one. I did get fish throughout the day, but those brookies of the dawn had really got me thinking. It was my first experience with spring creek fishing, and I knew nothing of midge larvae, cressbugs, and other stream minutiae.

Bill Pfieffer was the director of the Mont Alto Campus at that time, and a good friend of the legendary George Harvey. Bill was a consummate fly tyer and rather serious fly fisher, which is why I expect his posting to the Mont Alto Campus had been received with some gladness. It was not only a quiet life, but it was nearly on top of one of Pennsylvania's premier spring creeks. I'd taken a tying course from Dr. Pfieffer that winter, and he was always eager to help any of us with our fishing. I told him of the big brookies I'd seen, and he just laughed. It was my introduction to very small flies, the finest of tippets, and great care in presentation. It was also a chance to observe the way the fish used the weed beds as sheltering lies—I got broken off so many times.

It was this introduction to the world of the tiny that allowed me to fish Spring Creek just outside State College with confidence. It was in a local fly shop at the main campus where I found a box of gold-plated, size 28 hooks and tied my first adult midge imitations for the ultra-picky trout of the Fisherman's Paradise waters. It was not a little stream, but the lessons learned on tiny waters translated perfectly, and I took Spring's big browns on the smallest of dries.

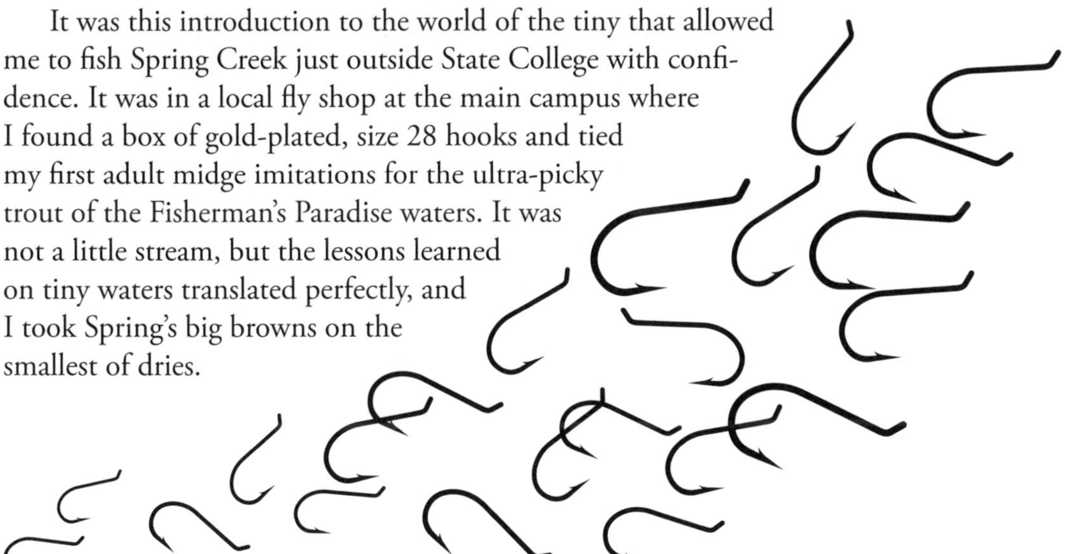

Black Earth & Mount Vernon Creeks

In graduate school at the University of Wisconsin–Madison, I quickly found Black Earth and Mount Vernon Creeks. Both are spring creeks, with a rich biology of insect life. Thick with aquatic vegetation, they flow through pasturelands where all manner of terrestrials find their way into their waters. Certainly in their main reaches, they are not little streams. In their upper couple of miles, they are no more that 15 feet wide, and so fall within the limits that I personally set on the definition of a little stream.

Richard Alden Knight's book, *Successful Trout Fishing* had just been published, and the idea of fishing dries downstream had immediate appeal to me. Perhaps it was all the downstream fishing I had done with the streamer in those little creeks in the hills around my parent's home, or perhaps it was just Knight's convincing arguments. Either way, it instantaneously galvanized me into fishing the dry down-and-across with action. This method proved especially effective, I noted, when I used it in places where there were eddy currents against the bank, where I needed to get a float back under overhanging vegetation, along the edge of an undercut bank, or on the upstream side of a fallen tree. There were many other lessons on those waters, and their stories will come later as we deal with reading larger waters and their more pronounced features.

Jason fishing a dry fly on California's Owens River using a Reach Mend to position the line down-and-across to help eliminate drag.

Costilla Creek & Number One Creek

We moved to Wausau, Wisconsin, in the late summer of 1971, and I began my professorial career at the University of Wisconsin–Marathon Campus. Within a year, I was given the opportunity of a lifetime when the Fenwick Rod Company asked me to become the Midwest Director of its newly established, national fly-fishing schools. Nancy taught in the schools with me, and Royce Dam, Bob Pils, Duane Stremlau, Arne Salli, Ed Knapp, Dave Engebretson, and occasionally others, rotated through as instructors. Jason attended every school, and learned how to cast and mend, tie knots, read waters, understand tactics, and identify the fish's food organisms (he also got in a lot of practice in the finer art of skipping stones).

In 1975, we were asked to set up schools on the Vermejo Ranch in northeastern New Mexico, west of Raton. Its 600,000 acres sprawl across the eastern slopes of the Sangre de Cristo Mountains, bordering on Colorado to the north and spilling out onto the desert lands toward the east and south. There are 27 fishable lakes on the ranch, and its streams are all little waters. One can step or jump across them for many of their miles, and they hold brookies, rainbows, and the somewhat rare, Rio Grande cutthroat. We added new instructors: Bob Pelzl and his wife Beverly, Dick Bloomershine, and Jim Aubrey, as well as rotating some of our other instructors from Wisconsin through the Vermejo schools.

Number One Creek and Costilla Creek are high-country streams, originating at over 10,000 feet, and threading their way through the open grasslands of the Costilla *vega*. They are bone-chillingly cold, and flow deep for their width. Because they flow through open country, one can approach them from any direction, depending upon conditions and needs. The fly-fishing schools we ran included one instructed fishing day, and the students worked both the lakes and the little streams. Students learned the upstream approach in the longer riffle areas, where they would crouch down and cast into likely spots from 30 feet away. We taught the across-stream approach on the larger pools, and had students develop their downstream skills in the sharp corners where the little streams snapped around to rush off in new directions.

Number One Creek on the Vermejo Ranch is a classic meandering, meadow stream; every corner is a pool with an undercut bank.

Though narrow, the depth of the streams gave them the character of much larger waters, and we could easily point out feeding lies at the tailouts and top edges of the pools, the riffles, and the shallower runs. We found prime lies largely in the corners, but there were culverts where logging and ranch roads crossed the streams, there were places where trees lay in the water, and there were undercut sod banks in some of the deeper runs. There were even a mini-few rapids with deep pockets that held fish. Because of the water's small size, the sheltering lies were basically all synonymous with the prime lies.

During the warm seasons, trout in the mountain meadow streams of the West feed heavily on terrestrial insects. Studies indicate that at least 50 percent of their food comes as "land fall." As a consequence, the students could use flies like a Royal Wulff or yellow-bellied Humpy and pull trout up with ease, and it was a simple matter to demonstrate feeding lies and prime lies with such eager fish.

Figure 3.1. *Setting up the Down Dry, Up Wet Tactic using a Parachute Mend: At the end of the casting stroke the rod is lifted back and up as the fly falls to the water. As the fly drifts down, the rod tip is lowered just a bit faster than the line is carried away.*

One of the tactics that we taught, a tactic that works anywhere, is the Down Dry, Up Wet. There were good populations of mayflies, caddises, and some stoneflies in the little streams, and because the fish were so surface conscious, they fell readily to this technique. We'd use an Elk Hair Caddis or Devil Bug and position the student upstream about 30 feet from a prime lie or suspected area containing feeding lies, and have them cast down, using a Parachute Mend—at the end of the casting stroke the rod is lifted back and up as the fly falls to the water, then as the fly drifts down, the rod tip is lowered just a bit faster than the line is carried away by the currents *(Figure 3.1)*. There were always a couple of eager fish ready to grab the dead-drifting dry.

At the end of the drift, the rod tip is given a sharp pull, low and to the side, to jerk the fly under water. Then the fly is fished back upstream with a series of short strips. Many times the biggest fish were taken on the wet retrieval. Wherever caddises are found, the fish will be used to seeing diving females, either headed down to lay eggs or headed back to the surface after ovipositing. The caddis patterns we selected would catch an air bubble when jerked under, giving the fly a look like the real egg-laying insect.

Both streams drained into Costilla Reservoir, and it held a good head of larger trout. A few of them found their way into the lower and mid-sections of the creeks, and occasionally a student would take a 14- to 16-inch brookie, rainbow, or cutthroat with the Down Dry, Up Wet Tactic.

Picking the Pocket

The little Vermejo streams contained much classic "pocket water" in their fast sections, although the pockets were miniature in size. In such streams, the pockets develop behind large rocks in the "rapids" sections. Pockets are the quiet water refuges for fish, and often each one will hold one or two trout watching eagerly for floating food. The fishing in such places can be fast and furious, or perhaps a better description would be "picking the pocket," quickly flicking a dry fly into the pocket, allowing a short float, and hoping for a fast rise. In such places, the fish cannot hesitate since the fly will be out of the pocket in a second or two.

In such waters—and there are many such places in small streams—the fishing is fast paced. I love to fish these waters with a short, fast action rod, a short leader to give instant turnover, and a high bobbing imitation like a Humpy, Goddard Caddis, Irresistible, or similar fly. The dry is dropped into the pocket, and the rod lifted to keep as much line off the swift currents as possible, while the fly dances alluringly on the calm waters of the pocket.

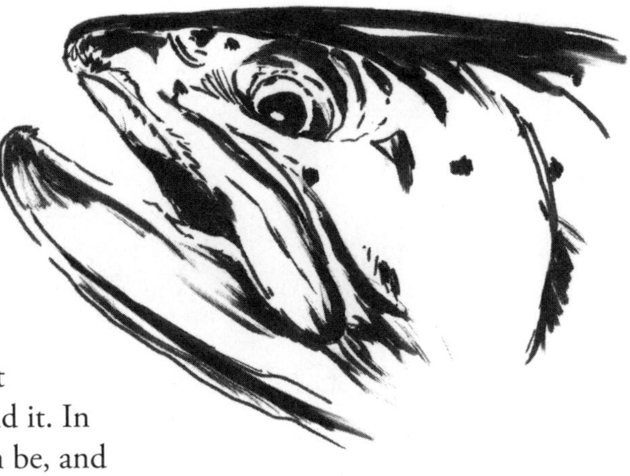

Pocket water is not just pocket water on small streams; it's pocket water on streams of every ilk. What differentiates it as pocket water is a slow current amidst a much larger expanse of fast currents; it is literally a "pocket" of water with a very different character than all the other water around it. In fast flowing rivers of any type, there can be, and usually is, pocket water.

And while there's nothing to hold one back from fishing pocket water on any stream, picking the pocket with a dry fly is especially gratifying on small to medium sized streams, where one can wade with relative ease and drop a dry into available pockets. In little streams the fish are usually small, but I have, on occasion, encountered some rather sizable beasts in such places. When a twenty-inch trout nails the fly in a stream that is only six feet wide, and then bolts downstream in the fast currents, the adrenalin kicks in. It's all a matter of perspective.

The Witte

One does not typically associate Africa with trout fishing, but there are certainly excellent trout waters at the continent's southern extreme. The Drakensberg Mountains and others in South Africa contain many streams whose cool waters support trout very nicely. The Witte tumbles down the highest valley in the Bain's Kloof Mountains north of Cape Town. Its wild browns are beautiful, if not plentiful. In its lower stretches, the

Witte is a river of pools. That is, the trout hold in the pools formed by house-sized boulders or where the water has dug its course along a rocky cliff. One finds an occasional big brown holding in the crystalline waters in this section.

A few hours' hike, however, puts the angler high in the shadow of the mountains' peaks, where the valley narrows, and the water, now truly a little stream, dashes through the rocks and stones. Like the fish of all small streams, the browns there are always on the alert for fast drifting food. They take the fly with a surprisingly quick rise. Because the water is mid-calf to mid-thigh deep, there are plenty of feeding lies and prime lies for the angler to explore. And, since the water forms basically one long, dashing rapids with pocket water, the fly fisher can work upstream with a short line, casting 20 feet or so with a series of rapid flicks (no false casting). It is fast, fun, and rewarding fishing in a rather spectacular setting.

The top end of the Witte is a continuous splash of pocket water where the fishing is a constant swift movement.

Dances with Riffles

While I grew up with small streams close at hand, and learned much from them and their trout, I did not fish them exclusively. In fact, I only fished them a few times each season. First, I didn't want to destroy the fish populations in these tiny waters, and second, I had Sugar Creek. It's a freestone stream of goodly proportions, a long throw across in some places, with deep waters—enough so that we had several "ol' swimmin' holes" well over six feet deep. It had real riffles and rapids, and long runs where we sometimes found surprising fishing. It was on Sugar Creek that reading waters became a full-blown reality for me.

Of special favor were the riffles. I loved the play of their water against my hippers, the tinge of danger when one got in near the top of one's boots, and, of course, the trout that I found there. In the early days, I used a spinning rod, six-pound mono, a size 10 or 12 hook knotted directly to the line, and a tiny split shot. Red wigglers, dug from beneath last year's composting manure pile, or perhaps a big crawler picked up on a rainy night, would be my bait of choice. I would dribble that wiggler or crawler through the darker slots in the riffles and nearly always manage to find a trout or two. Even those days were teaching times; now, whenever I fish a San Juan Worm, I am immediately cast back to those days of bait fishing.

Riffles are places where the stream is inclined and the bottom peppered with gravel, stones, and rocks. As kids we used to ask the differences among the three, and were told that gravel is too big to be sand, but too small to be stones. Stones are bigger than gravel, but not as big as rocks. And then, there are boulders, certainly bigger than rocks, and way to big to lift. Suffice it to say that there is a mixture of particle sizes with some of them being just a bit too big for a normal person to heft with ease.

Riffles are part of the natural language of freestone streams, as are pools, runs, flats, and rapids. Water coursing along a channel actually travels in a helical twist, and when it gets a toe-hold in the bottom, it can begin to gouge out the sand, gravel, stones and rocks. This is especially true during high-water periods. This load is carried for a short ways before it has to be dumped, forming riffles. As the years churn on, the stuff of riffles moves slowly down river. Some of it is eventually ground into sand. Other stuff marches on, having spent millennia in a quest for the sea.

Standing Waves

Rocks and other debris embedded in the bottom of riffles create a series of current obstructions. As the water strikes the face (upstream side) of the rocks, it is deflected upward. If the force of the current is sufficient and the water shallow enough, the upward thrusting water forms a standing wave at the surface. It's called that because it "stands" over the rock that forms it *(Figure 4.1)*. In fact, riffles, to really be riffles, have to have standing waves, otherwise they're just fast runs. In normal streams, it is unusual to see riffles more than about three feet deep, simply because the currents are not fast enough in deeper water to push much of a standing wave to the top. If the currents are so fast they could push waves that high, then they dig out the finer materials and become more rapids than riffles. Riffles can show white water when standing waves break, but not the rolling, boiling white water of true rapids.

The tune that riffles sing varies from "I got spurs that jingle, jingle, jangle" to the hustle and bustle of a New York City street over the noon-hour. The song that rapids

Figure 4.1. *Standing waves and generally shallow water are the trademark of riffles, like this fish-filled section of water in Alaska, where Ray Beadle fights a big rainbow.*

roar out is more like a heavy construction site with 'dozers, cranes, jackhammers, cement mixers, and more.

Riffles and rapids sometimes grade into one another, starting as a riffle, perhaps, and then roaring off as rapids, or visa versa *(Figure 4.2)*. They may alternate, as one sees on rivers like Montana's Madison. Rapids often contain gravel bars with riffle water surrounded by the heavy flows of the rapids.

Figure 4.2. *Riffles and rapids often grade into one another. This is a stretch of riffly rapids or rapidy riffles.*

I suppose one could grade riffles like we grade rapids—class 1 through 5—but for angling purposes, the important distinction is current speed and bottom composition: moderate currents, mostly stones and gravel with some larger rocks and even an occasional boulder = riffles. Plenty of big rocks, lots of white water that boils around the boulders and over the rocks, and very fast water = rapids.

Starting at the Top

Most anglers, seeing a riffle, want to wade right in and start fishing all that nice looking chop out there in the middle. Don't. Back off for just a second and have a good look. Fish may well be in the shallow edges, holding in feeding lies, and a quick-footed angler will spook them without ever seeing them. Make it a habit to look before you leap, in all angling situations.

One of the places that frequently holds feeding fish is at the very top of the riffle in the shallow seam formed along the edge of the fast water. The water at the outside of these seams may form a series of small reverse currents that spin out of the fast water. Close to shore, the water will be flat and seem totally uninteresting. It's the seam that is the key, so fish it before you wade it. On a straight riffle, there will be small reverses on either side of the stream; on a curving riffle, the reverse and flat water will be only on the inside edge. They may not look like much—in fact, let me make it a bit stronger, they

Jason landing the fish he's playing in the opening photo of this chapter, right where he hooked it—at the top, inside corner of the big riffle.

won't look like much—but they deserve your attention.

Dave Hughes tells a great story about fishing such places in his book, *Reading the Water,* and then goes on to say,

> "The corner of a riffle is usually only a foot or two deep. It is slightly rough on top, but not as choppy as the riffle outside it, and not as smooth as the backed up water to the inside. It is a transitional line of water, down along the edge of the riffle, that varies from about a foot wide to fifteen feet wide. It might extend for just a few feet, it might follow the riffle on down for fifty feet or so.
>
> It's amazing the number of fish you can draw up, even from the tiniest corner. You should absolutely never wade into a riffle until you have popped a few casts into the water that looks like it shouldn't hold any fish."

The Hydraulic Slip

Standing waves, the signature of the riffle, are good, and we'll come back to them in a bit, but let's look at the other side of the rock for a moment. The backside (downstream face) is in the lee of the current. In fact, the blockage created by the rock creates a hydraulic slip on the downstream side of the rock. A hydraulic slip is a place of calmer, protective water—a place where a fish can park and be out of the main current *(Figure 4.3).* Remember the number one rule for all fish lies: They must provide protection from currents.

Now, just for a moment, picture all the rocks on the bottom of a riffle. Any one bigger than about fist-size can create a hydraulic slip for a trout up to twenty inches in length. True, there won't be fish in every slip, and some slips are more desirable than others. The best ones, the ones that form prime lies, are in water more than knee deep and which have ready access to a current thread that carries food.

Bottom Variations

Occasionally a riffle will have stretches that are more or less equal in depth from one side to the other. If the water is deep enough, then the whole thing can be prime. But

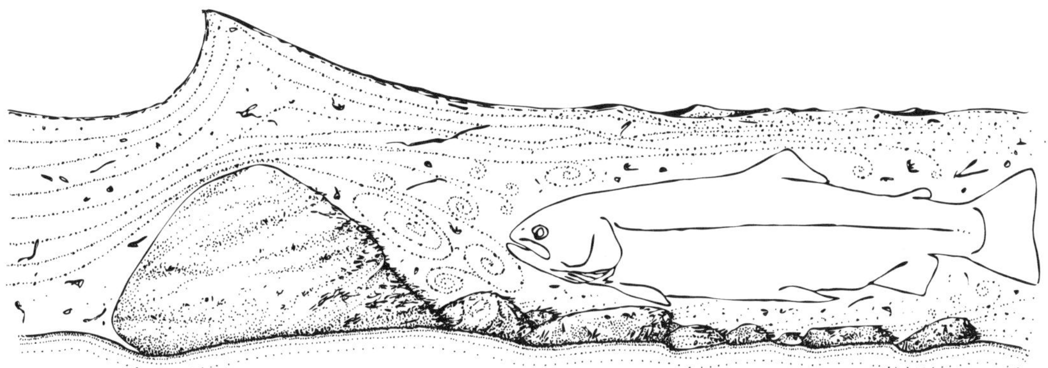

Figure 4.3. *Downstream of a rock is an hydraulic slip capable of protecting a fish from the currents.*

usually there are deeper and shallower areas in a riffle. Rarely is the deep section right in the very center because rarely is the stream a perfect "U" shape in cross section. The darkness of the water's depth, combined with the texture of the surface, will show such areas. If every area of a riffle were of equal depth and current speed, and the bottom made of uniformly sized rocks, then every standing wave would look like every other standing wave—all of the same height and curvature. But that's never the case. One area is obviously shallow, with slower currents, another area is faster and deeper with a more or less uniformly choppy surface. Another has some large standing waves, indicating big rocks close to the surface. Another area shows fast, dark (hence, deep) water and smaller standing waves; this area is deep enough to suppress the surface inflection of the standing waves.

But that doesn't mean that fish will only be in the deeper water. Fish might be in any and all these areas. The shallower water is certainly a place of feeding lies, and the deeper water certainly a place of prime lies. Larger rocks might offer prime water if the depth is there; otherwise they make good sheltering lies, if they are undercut at all. When in doubt, spend a few moments watching the shallower edges for feeding fish. If still in doubt, fish the water before wading in it. And whatever you do, don't tear into the prime water and wade right up the middle of it. Stay off to the side when possible and "wade" the best spots with your line and fly.

Riffle Slots

Quite frequently one finds riffles that have one or two deeper slots along part of, or all of, their length. And very often, these slots are more than knee deep. That's the place to really concentrate your efforts, because it's all prime water. However, don't neglect the other water in the riffle, especially if there's something going on that will draw fish into those areas. Fish hold in the prime lies because they offer protection and some grub on a regular basis, but when a hatch comes on, the fish disperse to feeding lies where they can better intercept floating food. In addition, as noted in the last chapter, in mountain meadow streams, trout will be out in the feeding lies watching for terrestrials all day long. Never rush a riffle.

One time I was invited to give a seminar at a fishing club in northern New Mexico. It was a great time, and the students were eager to learn. But then, as often happens when one teaches with enthusiasm, there came a challenge.

"After lunch we want you to show us this nymphing thing," one of the members said.

"Sure," I replied, "is there a good spot where everyone can watch?"

"The bridge," several of the members nodded, "that would a great place. The pool has got some big ones in it."

That got me excited. Then during lunch, one of the members told me that they wanted to see nymphing tactics because everyone there fished with dries. Now I was really excited. Talk about shooting fish in a barrel—or so I thought.

Lunch went quickly after that, and I was soon in my waders and vest, with my rod rigged, and heading for the water. Only about half the class was with me, so I figured we'd just stop at the bridge and talk through a variety of possible strategies while we waited for the others. Well, the others had different plans. They had gone directly to the bridge pool without passing "Go," or collecting their lunch. The pool was swarming with people, fishing from every angle. People in the water and people on the bank, all casting about and getting the trout in a decent state of panic for my presentation.

All was not lost, though. When I got to the bridge, I saw that the pool was fed by a nice long riffle that had enough depth to form prime lies. I gathered everyone from the pool and got them up on the bridge to watch my demonstration of nymphing with a split-shot and indicator. I figured that some pool trout may have slipped up into the riffle to get away from what was going on down below.

First, I demonstrated how to set up the nymphing rig. Then I explained what I would be doing and what they needed to watch for. I tied on a San Juan Worm, and walked down to the water. I noticed a darker slot of water over near the far shore and figured that there had to be fish in that slot. I stood at the edge of the riffle and pitched the fly upstream about 20 feet and into the head of the slot. It hadn't gone five feet before the indicator shot under and took off across the stream. Well, it certainly wasn't a snag, unless a 19-inch, rock-hard rainbow counts as a snag.

Fish number one was a very fine rainbow.

Landing the trout, I proceeded as if it was just another "normal" day of nymphing (after all, the pressure was now off). The next cast was a literal repeat of the first. After that fish was landed, the people on the bridge began to figit a bit. I yelled up and asked if anyone wanted to give it a try. Every hand went up, but I picked a guy who was totally new to fly fishing. I'd been talking with the students as we went through the casting practice, and he had admitted to never holding a fly rod before.

He came down, no waders, no vest, just his casual shoes and stood beside me on the shore. I let the line drag downstream and handed him the rod.

"Just lift the tip a bit," I coached, "and flip the rig upstream and into that darker water."

The fly landed near where my other casts had gone in, and the indicator shot under almost immediately. Nothing. He didn't even raise the rod tip. Not used to watching his line and leader, he hadn't even seen the indicator before it went under. I cocked the fly rod again, and this time, I told him I would let him know when a fish had taken the fly and when to set the hook. Again the fly plopped in and the indicator shot under.

"Set the hook!" I screeched as calmly as possible.

He set it all right. I'm surprised he didn't snap the fish's neck. Fortunately, everything held, and eventually, after some comedy and some white-knuckle moments, he got the 20-inch 'bow to the bank and released.

Nancy was fishing nearby, and to seal the deal, I called her over to fish the slot, while I stood on the bridge with the students and explained the tactic, step-by-step. She was using a Gold Ribbed Hare's Ear Nymph, and on the first cast, took the biggest fish of the afternoon.

After that, I didn't have to ask if anyone else wanted to try nymphing. I'm not sure that I even saw another dry fly for the rest of the day!

Riffle Pockets

Many times, riffle areas will have deeper pockets of water rather than, or in addition to, a long deep slot. And typically such places are prime, Just keep thinking, any riffle water more than knee deep is prime water. The late Charlie Brooks, whose book, *The Trout and the Stream*, is a very good study on reading waters in search of big fish, used to tell people who waded over knee deep into a riffle to get out because they were wading where the fish were. It's sage advice.

So, when fishing a riffle, always watch for deep-water pockets. They may not be as readily visible as a pronounced slot, but they will certainly hold fish, and often very nice ones. When we filmed *Nymphing* in 1982, we decided to shoot the whole thing on Armstrong Spring Creek. Its natural beauty was a factor, as was its configuration. There were riffles, slotted riffles, pocketed riffles, pools, runs, a pond, a slough, vegetation, and so on. It was (and still is) a good microcosm for the illustration of nymphing tactics.

When it came time to demonstrate the Shotgun Tactic, I chose to fish a section of riffle water that had several pockets. The stretch was at the bottom end of a long riffle, and it was a great place to set up a shoot that would illustrate the tactic. The Shotgun Tactic is used to fish nymphs in riffle water of more or less uniform depth with pockets and short slots. To demonstrate, I used my standard bottom bouncing nymph rig. In this case, the leader consisted of 4 feet of .020-inch Maxima Chameleon, 1 foot of .013-inch Maxima Chameleon, 4 feet of 3X tippet material, and 10 to 12 inches of 6X. The size 18 PMD nymph was at the terminal end of the 6X and one small split shot was clamped on just above the knot connecting the 6X to the 3X. An indicator was positioned five feet above the fly.

This was to be the first commercial instructional fly-fishing videotape, and to say there was pressure on me is a vast understatement. First, I had to catch fish more-or-less on command. We were shooting with 16mm film in those days, and paying a crew on a day-by-day basis. It was very expensive. There can't be too many mistakes, too many takes, too much waiting around, nor too much empty footage. That's one of the reason's I picked Armstrong Spring Creek. In those days, there were 5,000 trout per mile in the stream, and its hatches came like clockwork. I had already envisioned in my mind where each tactic would be shot, and how I would catch fish as efficiently as possible.

So, I'd picked the spot where I'd used the tactic with success many times before, and it worked just as well this time. The idea was to pick out a block of water about 10 x 10 feet upstream about 10 feet from my position, and then saturate that block with 20 to 30 casts before moving on to another section. Picking the 10 x 10 blocks was easy because each one encompassed a pocket in the riffle. I was able to wade in, explain the tactic, and catch fish quickly.

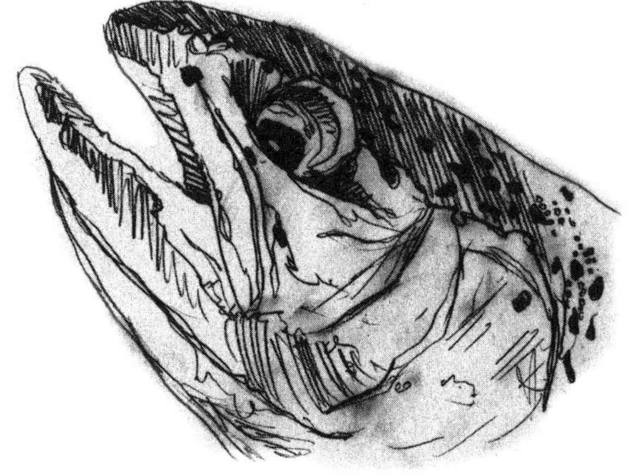

Ice Gouges

On my fist trip to Alaska in 1982, I fished out of the Gray Bow Lodge on the Talachulitna River. It was during the silver salmon run, and the fishing was excellent, not only for the salmon but for the hearty rainbows of the river, as well. In the evenings, we found graying rising abundantly in nearly every pool. I must confess that I only caught a few grayling because my focus was on the rainbows. I caught the salmon, to be sure, but when I had the chance to have a shot at the trout, I took it.

The very first day, I noticed that every riffle held large pockets, and that every large pocket held rainbows. Oh, there were plenty of 'bows in other spots, too, but there's something about drifting a big leech down a riffle with Joe Brooks' Broadside Float and seeing a big 'bow come out of one of those pockets and inhale the fly. Brooks developed the tactic for fishing streamers on big Montana rivers like the Yellowstone during the fall run of browns, but it works everywhere one finds trout.

The concept is easy, and the execution is also not too difficult. Cast up-and-across and then Reach Mend up. This positions the line nearly straight across. Then as the drift comes down, one lifts the rod tip and keeps it just ahead of the line. This keeps the extra slack picked up, off the currents. If the belly of the line starts to bow downstream, then the rod tip is merely flipped back up current to make a flopping, on-the-water mend.

A big leech-eating rainbow that was holding in an ice-gouge pocket in an Alaskan riffle.

This tactic works everywhere, but it is especially good in riffles because the dancing water makes the fly swim and twitch like a dying or disoriented minnow. And in the relatively shallow riffle water, the fly is readily seen by all nearby fish. I use this tactic often in Alaska. The broad waters require a lot of effort to cover efficiently. I start short and work further out with every two drifts. It has been my experience that fish will either take the fly on the first or second pass if they are in the mood to eat. I only lengthen the line about three feet to fish the next further slot. This way, if a fish wants to hit it on the third or fourth drift, the fly is still close enough to stimulate the fish. A note here: at the end of the drift, allow the fly to swing across the currents until it is straight downstream from you. Often fish will go after the swinging fly and nail it just as it straightens in the currents below your position.

When I quizzed our guide about the large pockets in the riffles, he explained that in the spring the ice would break up, and big sheets, several feet thick, would jam in the riffles, forming an ice dam. As the pressure of the water built, the dam would tear free. Blocks of ice would flip up on end, and the currents would push them along the bottom like a bulldozer blade. That's a great way to make rainbow habitat.

Riffle Reproduction

Not reproduction of riffles, but reproduction in riffles. Salmonids (char, trout and salmon) cut their nests, called redds, in riffle areas. Typically the female makes the redd by turning on her side and flipping her tail up and down sharply, right on the bottom. This movement lifts the bottom gravels and small stones, and the currents sweep them downstream for a foot or two. While she is doing this, the males are battling to establish breeding rights. She will repeat this many, many times over the course of several days before actually extruding her eggs with the male at her side extruding his sperm. Afterwards, the female moves upstream and repeats the whole process of lifting gravel into the currents so that it drifts down and covers the eggs.

It's strenuous work and many trout and Atlantic salmon don't survive it. Of course, all Pacific salmon die after spawning so that their decaying bodies can add nutrients back to the stream and promote growth of algae, insects, and bait fish for their young to eat before heading to the salt.

In those places where one can fish among spawning salmonids, go for the riffles, not deep slack-water pools. In the Lake States, fall runs of king salmon, cohos, pinks, and the hybrid pinooks (a cross between a pink and a king) with their associated runs

Below: Anglers hunting big kings in the Lake States do well fishing the riffles.

of browns and steelhead provide some great angling opportunities. The kings are fun because once they've been in the river for a week or so, the males get very aggressive and will eat streamers, leeches, and even egg flies. They fight hard, pulling string quite nicely. Sometimes one can find a steelhead just below a pair of egg-laying salmon and connect with a single egg fly or even a leech imitation.

As the kings wane into non-existence, the browns set up shop in the same places where the kings were playing house. They are aggressive fish, but very shy on sunny days, backing into deep water to retreat from their exposed positions in the riffles. On such days, I fish early and late. But I try to hit the water all day during overcast weather (even if it rains) because the fish stay in the riffles from dawn to dark. Getting into half-a-dozen browns in the 30-inch-plus range in a day can be fulfilling, to say the least.

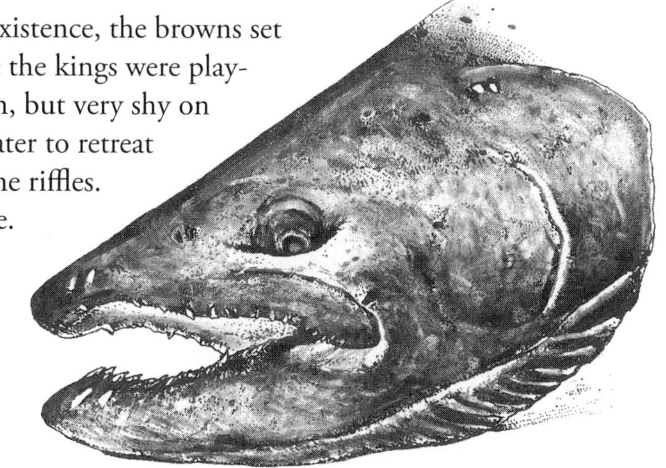

The reason we stalk riffly water in the tributaries of the Lake States during the salmon run.

But Alaska is the place to hit a spawning run of salmon, and fish for both them and the big rainbows. Kings start first in June, followed by sockeye, chum, pinks, and silvers. That's a whole summer and half of the fall filled with salmon just pouring eggs into every riffle in every stream. Trout will go from five pounds in the spring to seven pounds or more by the end of the salmon runs. They need the reserve to hold them over the long winter. They will eat an egg fly really well, too. But, they also take articulated leeches, mice flies, and, of course, the Egg Sucking Leech.

One summer I was in Alaska in late July. The sockeye were in, and they were abundant. More of them had made it through the "escapement period" than were anticipated. Every riffle was red with their brightly colored bodies. On this day, the staff at Iliamna Lake Lodge had awakened us early. The big lake (Iliamna) was particularly calm, they explained, and they'd be able to land a float plane at the mouth of the Gibraltar—not something they did very often due to the big waves that normally ruled the lake. We ate quickly, and were on the plane just as the sun began edging up in the eastern sky.

The lower end of the stream is a long, deep estuary with not much to read, but when we got to the top of it, I discovered something very exciting. That's a story for another chapter, though, so hang in there a bit longer. For now, back to the riffles. We moved up river fishing as we went. Eventually we came to a riffle that was at least half a mile long. It was very uniform in depth, with a few big boulders here and there, a few darker slots and pockets, and some fallen trees against the far shore.

It was absolutely alive with fish. In fact, we could hear them splashing before we actually came in sight of the riffle. It nearly took my breath away. As far as one could see, tails wagging in the air, water being splashed everywhere, and red bodies twisting and fighting. The big kype and bulbous nose of the male salmon create a gap in the fish's mouth that is the right size to fit around another male salmon's "wrist," the area just ahead of the tail (it's rightly called the caudal peduncle). When jousting with another male, a big salmon will grab its opponent by the caudal peduncle and shake violently, hoping to disable the other fish. It was in this riffle that I first observed this tactic, and not just once. Fish were sparring everywhere.

And then I noticed the gray forms, everywhere, too. I'd missed them in the chaos of the salmon. They were rainbows, and big ones. There weren't just a couple here and there, they were everywhere behind the paired salmon, and they were busy eating eggs.

I swung into action. I had been using a Gob-O-Eggs pattern quite successfully on this trip, and these trout loved it, too. It wasn't necessary to use an indicator, one could see the take clearly. The trick was to fish the Gob-O-Eggs on a long leader with a split-shot several inches above the fly, so that it bounced along naturally near the bottom. It was just like fishing riffles with a worm and shot when I was a kid. I was admittedly rather rude to those lovely, big 'bows. I was using 12-pound test Maxima Chameleon as a tippet, and there wasn't much "playing." It was more like "set-crank-land." When one knows how to fight fish, it's amazing how quickly they can be brought to hand under circumstances like those we encountered that day.

The shallow water and thousands of salmon made it hard for the 'bows to just blast off, and I didn't help them, either. I'd set the hook with a sideway strike, and then keep the fish coming by either stepping backward or stripping line like crazy. It may seem nuts to fight such big fish that way, but I wanted to get them in as quickly as possible

Below: THE Riffle.

in order to release them as fresh as possible (and to get another!). I realized that I might never see such a concentration of big, wild rainbows again in my lifetime, and I wanted to make the most of it. My premonition was indeed true. I have fished Alaska many times since that day, but I've only had one other time that even came close. Look for it in Chapter Six.

Riffle Distortions

Fly fishers have a couple of distinct advantages in riffle water. First, fish can't see the angler very well, and second, they can't hear the angler very well. In riffle water, the fish's window is broken into a series of ever-changing holes, with a more-or-less clear opening directly above the fish. Thus the image of a close angler, which would normally be quite easy to discern by the fish, is a mess of blotches: cut up, squashed, stretched out, and rather unrecognizable. To the fish, the angler is part of the highly perforated, and always changing zone at the edge of the window. Part of this edge is reflecting bottom objects like rocks, while part of it is showing flashes of sky. The broken blobs of the angler's image fit right in with everything else that's going on.

A nice rainbow from THE riffle; it took a Gob-O-Eggs.

This means that the fly fisher can get quite close to the fish before there's a sense of predator recognition. That's why the Shotgun Tactic works so well with its short casts. That's why Czech nymphing is so deadly right off the end of the rod tip.

The "sound" that predators make as they move through the water consists of displacement waves (also called "pressure waves"). These "sounds" are picked up by the fish's lateral line, which is highly sensitive to the slightest variations in water motion. But in riffles, there's a huge amount of "background" noise that effectively blocks the fish's sensitivity to all but the most powerful waves—like those created by an angler crashing upstream in haste to get to the "best" spot. Many times, in spite of knowing better, I've waded into a riffle to cross the stream or to hasten to fish rising in a pool above and flushed out big fish. I was so close to them when they dashed off that I could have literally stepped on them. This is a rather powerful (yet self-condemning) illustration of how much riffle waters can block the fish's vision and hearing.

So, just because the fish can't hear you well, or easily make out your chopped up image, don't wade recklessly. Take your time and pay attention to what's going on. I've done the careful thing and spotted big fish, then backed off and caught them. As in all predatory endeavors, the less the prey knows about the predator the better.

Fly Selection for Riffles

Riffles are the biological hotbeds of the stream. First, the water is relatively shallow, and so the full spectrum of sunlight reaches the bottom. Plants use red and blue light most strongly for photosynthesis, and in riffles they get both. In the bottom of a six-foot deep pool, there wouldn't be any red light; it would have all been absorbed by the water above. Second, the surface area of the rubble bottom is very large, providing a vast space for algae growth. Third, the spaces between the rocks provide great cover for insects and other food organisms, including sculpins, worms, and if there's some rooted vegetation,

In heavy riffles such as these, the fish have a very difficult time seeing and hearing the angler, allowing my wife, Nancy, to take fish right off the tip of her rod.

scuds, cressbugs, and other critters. Fourth, the water in the riffles is highly oxygenated from all the wave action. No wonder fish want to be there.

This abundance of food and the relatively shallow depths of a riffle mean that during opportunistic times, anglers can use just about any fly that they enjoy fishing. I have friends that only want to catch trout on dries. Guess where they like to fish the most? On the Bighorn, I fish cressbug imitations with great effect in the riffles, but flies tied to suggest midge larvae, scuds, smaller mayfly nymphs, and caddis larvae all do well, too. Then again, I may fish a Griffith's Gnat or Elk Hair Caddis, or perhaps a Dry and Dropper combo. Perhaps I'll rip a big sculpin or leech imitation over the gravel. And these work on all riffles, not just those on the 'Horn.

Pool Parts

Pool Morphology

In classic stream morphology, riffles/rapids and pools alternate, leap-frogging their way to the sea. Riffles are shallow, have coarse bottom sediments (usually rocks), and have relatively swift moving water. Pools are the opposite in all regards: They're deep, have more fine bottom sediments (sand, silt, mud), and have relatively slow moving water. In fact, by definition, pools are the deepest areas in a stream. Riffles are easy to read because the swift, shallow water forms standing waves above the larger bottom objects. But in pools, the combination of slow currents, greater depth, and finer bottom sediments creates a rather uniform, smooth surface that reveals little about potential holding lies. However, with just a bit of understanding about the overall structure of pools, the fly fisher can quickly be fishing these waters.

All pools can be divided into four zones *(Figure 5.1)*. **Zone one** is the head of the pool. It's the areas where the currents slow dramatically as they tumble out of the riffle into the depths of the pool. **Zone two** is the belly or body of the pool. It's the slow, flat water in the pool's center and is usually the deepest area of the pool. This is a great refuge for fish, and one can find them here almost anytime. The deep slow waters are a great place to fish a sculpin imitation on a sinking line with a slow, hand-twist retrieve. Nymphs fished on a long leader with a suspending indicator will produce fish in zone two. And on occasion, I have had great dry fly fishing in the belly of the pool when the surface has been alive with hatching or egg-laying insects. **Zone three** is made up of the edges of the pool, which are often shallow, but perhaps not, as we shall soon see. Edges are not places to be neglected, though many fly fishers view then as only a convenient wading zone. **Zone four** is the tailout. It's the downstream end of the pool where the currents gather themselves for another wild ride through the riffles or rapids below. The tailout is usually the shallowest area of the pool proper.

In classic river formation, pools alternate with riffles or rapids.

Zone One: The Head

The head of the pool usually displays three distinct features (1) the throat, which represents the currents that rush in at the top. The throat extends downstream to the point where the currents flatten out. (2) One or two reverse currents that form at the side(s) of the throat. (3) The transition in depth from the shallower water of the riffle/rapids to the deep waters of the pool, caused by the change in the profile of the stream bottom. There is often a rather abrupt change in depth, going from perhaps a few feet deep in the fast stretch to several more feet deep, quite quickly. This abrupt transition in depth is called the "lip" of the pool.

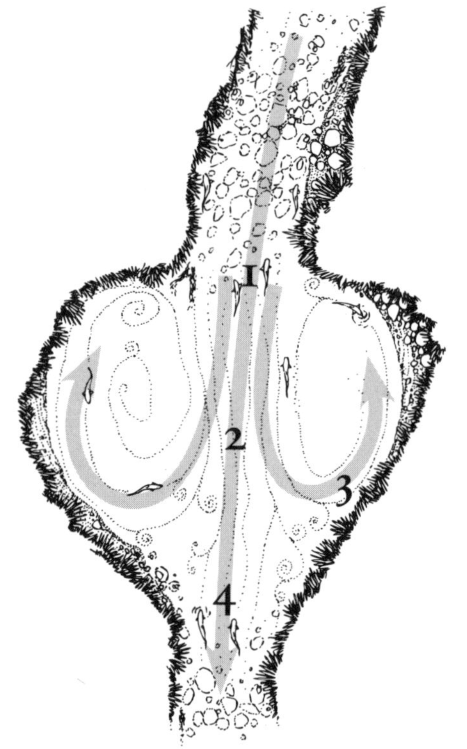

Figure 5.1. *In the classic pool, the head is fed by a riffle. The fast water extends into the pool a ways to form the throat. Reverse currents form on either side. The deep belly of the pool feeds into the tail-out of the pool that dumps into the riffle below.*

The Throat

The throat of the pool can have a variety of configurations, The currents that rush in may be fast, extending the throat a fair distance into the pool's belly. They may be slow, and extend only a couple of yards before the surface flattens. The throat might be very narrow or quite broad, of great depth, or very shallow. Lots of possibilities, so potentially an area of feeding lies or prime lies, depending upon water depth.

Figure 5.2. The throat extend a ways into the pool, depending upon the speed of the water entering from the riffle or rapids above. Here, my friend, Mike Allen, is fishing the edge of the throat (dashed line) in a New Zealand stream.

Of course, fishing along the bottom in the throat currents can be effective, especially at the edges of the strong central current tongue where it interacts with the slower, usually reverse currents, at the sides *(Figure 5.2)*. During a hatch or egg laying period, there are often fish feeding at the film in these areas.

Often times, in the big pools of steelhead rivers, the throat is an excellent place to find parked fish. They can hang in the highly oxygenated water, along the bottom and out of the currents, and prep for the next leg of the journey. But the throat is not just for staging steelhead. Any and all anadromous species will hang in bottom currents of the throat as a staging area *(Figure 5.3)*.

Figure 5.3. *The "soft water" just to the inside of the throat is a great place to find resting steelhead.*

The Lip

The head of the pool is the area of greatest food influx because it catches all the drift from the riffle or rapids above. Thus, fish will often move to the head of the pool to feed. The fish hold in the throat and just downstream of the lip, under the fast water rushing in from the riffles *(Figure 5.4)*. In this position, they can stay out of the heavy currents, but are still within striking range of any drifting food items. If the water at this position is less than knee deep, then this area is a feeding lie. That is, fish will go there to

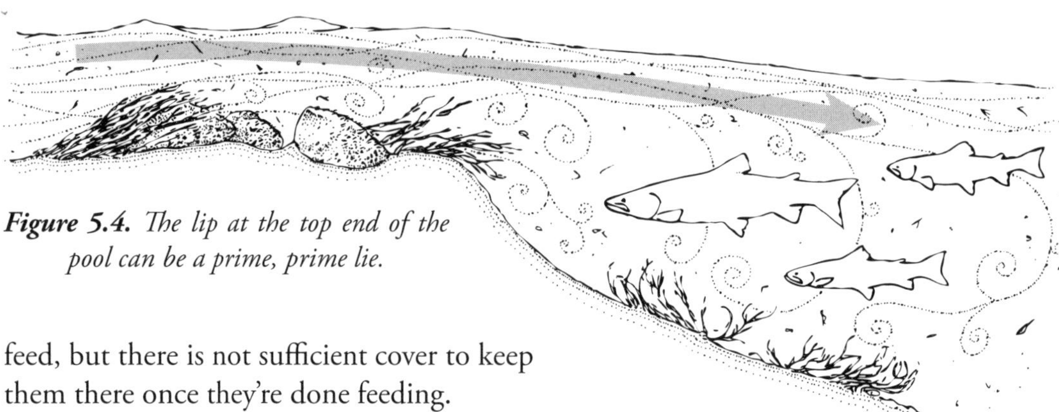

Figure 5.4. *The lip at the top end of the pool can be a prime, prime lie.*

feed, but there is not sufficient cover to keep them there once they're done feeding.

If the fast water just upstream of the lip is more than knee deep, then this area is a prime lie. And it's one of the best the stream can offer. It has both food and protection from predators, and fish will hold there continually. These are the places you need to seek out, because they concentrate the fish, and there will usually be some in feeding mode.

Jason and I spent a couple of weeks fishing for huge browns on Russia's Kola peninsula and shooting a couple of TV shows. Filming is always difficult because of weather, the amount of gear that has to be dragged around, the need to get into fish quickly, and so on. On one of the rivers the chopper put us down next to a long, lake-like pool. Rather than waste time fishing the center reaches for the occasional fish that might be cruising there, we marched right to the head and immediately began taking fish at the lip—big fish, too, I might add.

If the water at the head position is more than waist deep, then this area will be a good nymphing or long fly area, but not usually a good dry fly area. The fish will not usually come up through all that fast water to take a tiny surface morsel. Then, too, it's hard for them to see a tiny object that far away in all that fast chop. However, if there are big insects (like *Hexagenia* mayflies or big stoneflies), or maybe a mouse on the surface, then the fish will put out the energy needed to get a big mouthful like that.

When Jason was ten years old, we fished a big pool on Wyoming's Green River. The water poured into the pool, forming a dark drop off at the lip, where the bottom fell away sharply. I showed Jason where to position himself and how to place the big, black Strip Leech so it would sink deep and sweep across the bottom just at the lip. On my fist cast, I hooked and landed a nice 17-inch brown. Just to be sure Jason had clearly understood my instructions, I demonstrated again and on this second cast took an 18-inch brown. These were nice fish, but neither Jason nor I thought they were monsters. Jason had been fishing for big trout for five years by that time and had caught plenty of them in that size range. Their abundant presence, however, did get our hopes up.

Jason made a couple of tentative casts that didn't reach the mark, and I pointed out the need for more distance and a better mend. On the next cast he got it right, and I turned to walk away. There was a loud splash behind me, and I turned, thinking perhaps Jason had slipped and fallen in. He hadn't. The rod tip was bowed to the surface, and he strained back hard against a big fish. The water was deep and the current heavy, so I grabbed the back of his vest and steadied him as he moved down with the brown. I kept assuring him that it wasn't "that big," and that he should play it like any other 20-incher. He knew better, and there was a bit of panic in his voice as he replied, "Okay."

The fish moved down into the deep water at the belly of the pool and hugged the bottom, holding in the best sheltering lie the pool offered. But Jason's relentless side pressure kept it off balance, and finally the fish decided to leave the pool. It headed off downstream, toward a surging rapids below. I got Jason to the shore, and he ran after the big brown, keeping strong side pressure the whole time. I ran down in the water behind Jason, waiting my chance. Jason finally got the brown close to shore and saw its size. That made him all the more determined, and he really bent the rod to force the fish in close. At the right monent, I scooped it up with a surging, two-arm grab, getting completely soaked in the process.

It was a third-of-a-mile downstream from the hook-up point when I finally hoisted the huge brown ashore. At 25 inches and over 6 pounds it was the biggest fish of Jason's young life.

Jason with his youthful prize, taken from the lip of the big pool behind him.

On another trip years later, Duane Stremlau and I had driven from Wisconsin to Montana's Bighorn River in one day's *looong* push, and we were ready to catch fish. After a night filled with dreams of blue, big Montana skies, we awoke bright and early to cold, pouring rain. Mike Craig, a friend and owner of the Bighorn Angler at the time, gave us a wry smile and a somewhat sheepish look as we stumbled into the shop a half hour before dawn.

"It's supposed to rain like this all day," Mike apologized. "I'll drop you off wherever you want, if you want."

"We came to fish, and we've got plenty of gear," I said. "Just drop us at Three-Mile."

The water was perfect, as it nearly always is in that tailwater fishery. Nothing was hatching that we could see, and there were no bank sippers or even rises from little fish. I knew the river, and so I told Duane to jump in the drift boat, and we'd head downstream. We pulled into the back channel behind an island, and clambered out. Duane immediately hit the turbulence line where the back channel intersected the main stem. Such places are certainly prime lies if they are more than knee deep, and that one was.

As he was getting into position and rigging up, I walked up to the top of the back channel pool and flipped a nymph in just above the lip. I used a Curve Mend so the fly landed downstream of the line and leader. This way, the fly would plunge, uninhibited by drag, right down over the lip into the deep water on its downstream edge. The indicator shot under even before the line came tight. It was a nice 17-inch brown.

Well, every brown in the river must have been in that spot. Duane and I literally fished it until 3pm, when we had to jump in the boat and row the nine miles down to the takeout. We never bothered to count fish; neither of us wanted anything to potentially ruin one of the best days of nymphing we've ever had.

Okay, now back to the Gibraltar. I promised in the last chapter to finish the story about that river, so here it is. Picking up where I left off, I was with a group of friends right at the river's mouth. As we were walking up the estuary area, I kept looking in its deep dark waters, but saw nothing. When we got to the top end, I stopped to watch the lip for a while, hoping a rainbow or two might be there.

The others went on to the top of the first riffle above the estuary and began fishing. As I continued to watch the lip, I noticed that the bottom was moving a bit. I didn't think a thing of it. Water, after all, moves and swirls and often gives the impression that the bottom is moving around. But, no, there it was again. Somewhat perplexed, but at the same time suspicious, I plopped the Gob-O-Eggs just above the lip with a

Curve Mend so the fly landed downstream of the line and leader (you may have already guessed that this is one of my favorite tactics for fishing a sunken fly down over a lip).

This time I could see the fluorescent red imitation disappear in the mouth of a nice rainbow. I played the fish aggressively, flipped the barbless hook out, and tossed the fly right back to the same spot. If what I thought I had seen when I hooked that first 'bow was true, I was going to catch some fish.

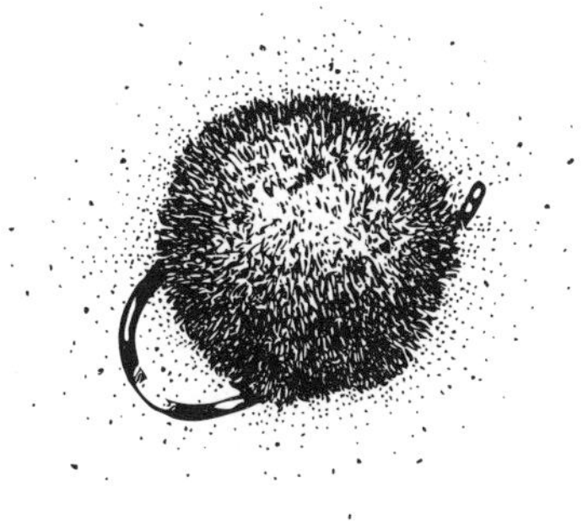

Well, it never stopped—for three hours. The big 'bows just kept coming. It was better than shooting fish in a barrel, I was catching them in a barrel. They were dumber than a sack full of hammers, too, and far more cooperative than I had any right to expect.

Finally, my other companions came back looking for me. I didn't want to leave. The bottom of the pool was black with trout; I'd never seen anything like it, and certainly didn't want to leave it. But, we had to catch the floatplane late that afternoon several miles up stream, and I just couldn't stay any longer if we were going to fish our way up. I've never found anything like that since, though I look every chance I get. The bows were following the sockeye and had staged at the top of the pool. As it turned out, there were thousands of eggs washing down, and those fish were just eating themselves silly. But then, there were those riffles upstream....

It would be easy to fill the remainder of this chapter and several more with illustrations of fish pulled off the lip at the head of a pool. Let's just leave it with the note that this is one of the best prime lies in the whole river. Give it everything you've got.

Certainly there are pools that do not have a strongly pronounced lip at the top end; rather they simply get gradually deeper. Even so, don't neglect this top end area. It's still the major source of food for the pool and it can be a great feeding zone. In addition, there may be other features that are discussed below that will encourage fish to occupy the area.

Reverse Currents

The head of the pool is also the place of reverse currents. These cyclonic sweeps of water may be only a foot or two across in a small stream, but can be a hundred feet of more across on huge rivers. They're caused by water pressure differentials along the length of the pool. At the top of the pool the in-racing, fast water has less internal pressure than the slower water lower down in the pool (Bernoulli's principle). Therefore the water pushes outward at the bottom of the pool (increased pressure) and is drawn into the fast water at the top *(see Figure 5.1)*.

Food items trapped in these reverses stay trapped for long periods, and so a reverse can concentrate food. During a heavy hatch, for example, a reverse current can be literally jammed with the bodies of floating insects. Well, where food is concentrated, the fish concentrate. One of the rules of reading waters is that "Fish Follow Food." So anyplace that concentrates currents, concentrates food, concentrates fish.

If the reverse is big enough and deep enough, it will hold fish. Less than knee deep the reverse will be a feeding lie; more than knee deep, it will be a prime lie. Always give such places a careful look before moving on. In fact, give them more than a look; fish them hard.

Reverses can set up anywhere there are current differentials. One finds them in riffles, rapids, and runs, too. Typically in riffles, the reverses are simply small swirling currents at the edges. They can suck insects off the main current and provide a food chain for feeding lies. We'll look at them in rapids and runs in Chapter Seven. There are more notes on reverse currents in pools below.

Zone Two: In the Pool's Belly

The belly of the pool is one of its sheltering lies. A sheltering lie is *under* something, and out there on the bottom, the fish is under a lot of water. Very often when one hooks a fish in the shallow edges, up in the throat, or down at the tail, the fish's first response is to head for the deepest part of the pool. When the line comes tight, and the fish feels that pressure, it runs off to a sheltering lie (or the shelter of a prime lie). Knowing that this will be the fish's response is the first step in understanding how to fight fish (much more on the strategies of fighting fish in our forthcoming book, *The Angler as Predator*).

The fishing in the belly of the pool may or may not be any good. It depends on water depth, the shape of the pool, the presence of vegetation, bottom structures, and any bank structures that might provide cover. In smaller streams, where the only water

Nancy connects with a nice trout in the belly of the pool on a small, Colorado stream.

of any depth is in the pool's belly, the entire belly may be one giant prime lie. In fact, it may be the *prime*, prime lie. On small streams the water at the head of the pool and in riffles, flats, and other stream features is usually too shallow to form prime lies. Feeding lies yes, but prime lies, no. For example, on many of the small- to medium-sized streams in Alaska, rainbows will frequently hang out all along the length of the pools. These are usually faster water pools that may drop off to depth gradually, or pools where there's plenty of fallen trees, brush, and grasses to offer protective, overhead shelter.

One summer, my friend, Dave Graebel, and I were fishing the far upper reaches of the Brooks River in Alaska with John and Matt Holman from No-See-Um Lodge. Dave loves to catch 'bows on dries, and he was getting his share. I wanted to find out where the fish were holding and get an idea of the numbers of fish in that stretch of the river. So I hung a big articulated leech on the end of my 15-pound tippet and began to search as vigorously as I could. I moved quickly because the fish either wanted the big fly or they didn't, and casting to the same spot more than once was a waste of time. When the 'bows are turned on, the fishing can be really good—and this day they were turned on!

I came to a long, straight pool that was deep along the far bank and gradually got shallower toward my side. It was a great place to wade along and toss the fly back under the overhanging tree branches into the dark water. I took over a dozen big rainbows from the belly of that pool, one group of seven in seven casts.

On the other hand, on huge waters, where the belly is very deep and slow with wide shallow edges, it may be hard to locate any feeding fish unless there's something to get them out into feeding lies. Although there will be fish in the deepest waters, they are usually quite spread out, Probing the very deep, bottom of the pool can sometimes be successful, but in such big rivers, it's usually more productive to seek specific feeding areas or prime lies. We'll look at some instances below.

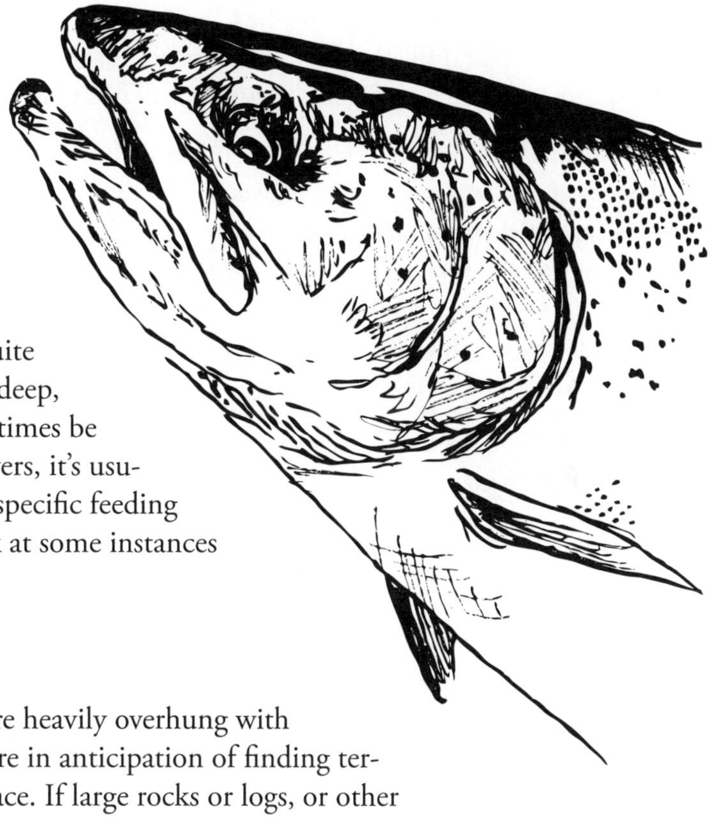

Zone Three: Pool Edges

If the edges of the pool are heavily overhung with vegetation, fish may hold there in anticipation of finding terrestrials that drop to the surface. If large rocks or logs, or other

Dave Graebel fighting a nice brown that was feeding just at the edge of the overhanging vegetation along the left-hand bank of this pool.

bottom obstructions rise near to the surface, they can be places where fish will hang out, too. Edges can be deep, or they may be shallow. When they're shallow, they're feeding lies, but if there's depth, then it will be prime water. In the pool on the upper Brooks, one side was deep and filled with fish, the other side was shallow and offered easy wading. It didn't take much to make the correct interpretation in that case.

But what about hatch periods? Often fish will drift out into the shallow waters of pool edges and set up feeding lies in water no more than a few inches deep. I've walked over enough of them to have finally learned this. It pays to watch the shallow side when there's food to move the fish. Even if the food isn't on top, there may be drifting eggs, nymphs, larvae, pupae, scuds, cressbugs, worms, stonefly nymphs crawling to shore, sculpins flitting around on the bottom, and so on. This is especially true in the twilight of dawn and dusk, and in the after-dark hours.

Then there are the edges on corner pools. Very often the outside edge is undercut or dug into the bank with a series of gouges and lumps and bumps that can offer protection from currents. It always surprises me how small a bank projection can be and still offer a lie. When I'm floating and fishing along a bank, I hit every spot I have the opportunity to get a fly into, no matter how seemingly insignificant. We'll look at edges a bit more carefully in association with the pools discussed in Chapter Six.

Zone Four: The Tailout

The tailout is a feeding zone. Its shallow waters make it easy for the fish to watch the surface. During a hatch, very large fish may back out of the pool's belly and feed quietly

Look familiar? The lead-in photo for this chapter was taken in the tailout (lower half shown) of a big pool in New Zealand. A large rainbow hooked along the edge of this tailout did what fish generally don't do—it immediately turned and headed down into the fast water below, forcing me to run after it.

in the tailout. I've taken many good fish in the tailouts of pools the world over. Because the water is thin, the fish are spooky, so approach such areas with great caution and cast very carefully. This is one place where I greatly prefer to use a downstream approach so that I'm not tossing line up onto the slow tailout from the faster riffle water below. The shallow tailout also invites the presence of forage fish, crawfish, leeches, and other food items, and so this area is a favorite haunt for night feeding browns. A fish that is hooked here will generally run up into the deep water at the pool's belly.

Interestingly, over the years, I've also both read and heard the term "lip" applied to the very end of the tailout—at the point where the water leaps over into the riffles or rapids below. I guess, if fly fishing were a bit more humorously oriented, we'd call these the upper lip and lower lip.

The very end of the tailout, just before the lip, is a great place for a migrating fish to rest after its run through the fast water below. It's also a great place for them to spawn. The press of the pool's water forces it to flow down into the gravel at the top of the riffle or rapids. This is something the spawning fish look for. In the Lake States, that's one of the first places I look to see what's going on relative to fish numbers and sizes, be they salmon, browns, or steelhead. It seems that the biggest fish usually grab this most ideal spawning place. So if there are plenty of fish, and big ones right at the very end of the pool, hanging right on the lip, I know it's going to be good fishing. I've caught literally hundreds of fish off the lip of the tailout. My biggest lake-run brown to date came out of just such a place.

Scour Pool

Technically, all pools are "scoured" out of the channel by the currents, but what I have in mind here are those pools formed where pools would not normally be formed by an uninhibited current flow. A scour pool might be formed in the center of a riffle, for example, when a tree falls into the stream and dams the swiftly flowing currents. The currents quickly dig a deep slot under the obstruction *(Figure 5.5)*.

When a scour pool is formed by a log lying at an angle to the currents, you can be certain that it's a great place for fish to hang out. Great because the upstream lip of the scour pool is like the upstream lip of any pool, and because the log provides overhead cover for the fish. Then again, such pools are not so great—not so great for the angler because it can be exceedingly difficult to get a fly into the prime water without getting hung up on the log (and usually all the other flotsam that accumulates on the log). Such places still deserve a good try or two, though.

My favorite time to fish scour pools is when there is surface activity to get the fish on top. At such times, the best fish may drift downstream and hold in the tailout to feed. Be warned, however, when hooked they go for the cover of the log at full speed.

Figure 5.5. *A scour pool formed by a log lying partially across a fast riffle.*

Fishing Pools

All pools have the same basic anatomy that we discussed in the last chapter. Beyond that, pools can be categorized basically by their shape. And while, overall, all pools have a head, reverses, belly, edges, and tailout, each shape offers something unique to the fly fisher. Understanding these unique features helps the angler to take full advantage of all the feeding lies and prime lies that pools offer.

Straight Pool

This is the classic pool that most of us envision when we hear the term "pool." Riffles drop in at the top, the pool swells out to the sides, and is perhaps a bit longer than wide. A reverse current is set up at either side of the inflow. Foam drifts down the length of the slow belly of the pool and into the tail. The tailout bows downstream into the top of the next set of riffles. I must admit that I know a few pools like that. But for every one of these classic straight pools, there are perhaps a dozen other straight pools that vary from this norm; in pools, the exception seems to be the rule.

Perhaps the most common variant is a straight pool that is deeper along one side than the other, like the one I mentioned in Chapter Five that Dave Graebel and I fished on the Brooks in Alaska. There was another special pool like that on the Moraine in Alaska. Bo Bennet was the chief pilot for Kulik Lodge at that time, and he had flown Ray Beadle, Ed Rice, and me into Cross Winds Lake as early as we could get in there under VFR conditions. Ed headed straight cross-country to the stream; Ray and I headed down river a couple of miles. We approached the river from the top of a very high bluff at the head of a big pool. It was a great spot to see every inch of the water. Smaller fish would not have been easy to see, but those we saw certainly were visible. They were stacked in the top end of the pool like cordwood. Even now, when I write this, I get the mental image of that morning. The air was crisp, clean and fresh. The sun was just poking up over the mountains to the east. And there below us was a long, straight pool whose top end was filled with big, healthy rainbows. The fish were there to eat sockeye salmon eggs and decaying salmon flesh.

We worked our way downstream to a place where the land sloped more invitingly, and made our way to the water. The shallow side of the pool was waist deep; even then it was a long cast to the big fish on the deeper side. Fortunately, when one had waded out, there was plenty of unhindered backcast room, and it was easy to punch out long casts. I was fishing the Gob-O-Eggs with a split shot a foot above it. On the very first cast, a big rainbow inhaled the fly and bolted off, down the deep-water belly of the pool. We fished over the 'bows until noon when the action slowed, and then we moved down. Below the pool was a strong rapids, but we walked past it; the fish were in the pools. Or maybe not—the story continues in the next chapter....

The big pool on Alaska's Moraine River where Ray and I found a large school of big rainbows just waiting to eat our flies.

Now, let me make a note here. When I was fishing the Gibraltar and encountered all those big fish, I was able to land them quickly because I was fishing a short line and could run around at will, allowing me to rapidly get control of the fish's head. But when one is standing mid-thigh deep in the river, and it's 50 feet back to the shore, and the cast is long, the fish has plenty of time of rip around before the angler gains control. In this case, it was 60 feet or more to the fish, and that gave them plenty of room to maneuver. So, when they'd run, I'd have to let them go and stand still to fight them. Of course, that's part of the fun, too. Each circumstance offers its own unique opportunities and angling satisfactions.

One of the big rainbows from the Moraine.

Confluence Line, Turbulence Line, Seam

Straight pools have two reverses, one on either side of the fast water that is coming in. In the case of the Alaskan pool above, the reverse on the shallow side was too shallow, and nothing was in there. There were fish across the fast water in the confluence line on the deep side, however. The confluence line *(Figure 6.1)* is the choppy water that sets up where the waters of the reverse cycles into the main current. The co-joining of the currents sets up turbulence, so the confluence line is also a turbulence line. Just keep

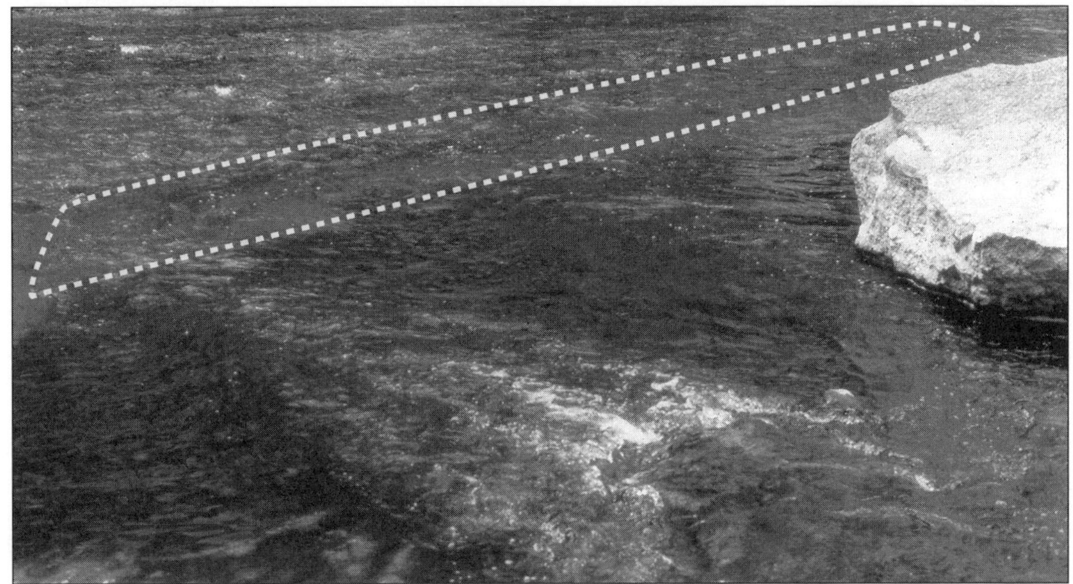

Figure 6.1. *The confluence of currents creates a distinct seam where they mix.*

this in mind when reading waters: *turbulence lines mean slower currents.* It's a place where fish can hang out and look for grub with minimum expenditure of energy. A confluence line is also a seam; that is, a demarcation line between currents of different speeds. More on variations on the seam theme in the next chapter.

If the water in a confluence line is more than knee deep, it should be considered a prime lie—and a good one. I was fishing the Babine, again with my fishing friend, Dave Graebel, and the guides put me on a long straight pool with a moderate-sized stream entering on the far side. I was glad for the double-handed rod, because right behind me, too close even for classic Spey casting, was a very high gravel bank. I had to use a variation known as a Perry Poke, in which the line is dumped directly in front of the angler, and the "D" loop is formed in a relatively forward position. It's quite effective, and after the guides showed me this cast, I used it exclusively.

I worked down the big pool, tossing as much line as I could, reaching the deep water along the far bank. No fish had run up the river in the last week or two, and everyone in camp was experiencing slim pickin's, so I worked as hard as I could down this perfect water. Nothing. Then I came to the confluence line. I could see the water boiling and grinding where the flow of the side stream was integrated into the main currents. I had my sights on this spot, and fired a long toss into it. The Type-V sink-tip shot under, pulling the purple Hot Head Leech with it.

The fly's hook point was missing, giving the fish a distinct advantage.

With steelhead, one rarely has to wonder if the strike is a strike—and I had a strike. I set with determination, and the line peeled off the reel as the fish shook its head and quickly countered the pull of the rod. It was easy to tell by the signals that it telegraphed to me that the steelhead was big. I reeled and held fast. I began easing down the bank, but the going was tough. Round rocks, all about the size of a bocce ball, rolled and tumbled away from under my feet. I could feel the fish give a mighty surge, and then it jumped, high. I could see the fly in the corner of its mouth, and I could see every black dot on its side. The fish hit the water, and the line went slack. I reeled in. The fly was still there. Checking the point, I discovered there wasn't one. The hook had broken right at the barb. Ah, well, I was going to release it anyway, but it would have been fun to see how much over twenty pounds it would have gone.

Once, when Nancy and Jason and I were fishing in Yellowstone, we pulled into a turnout and stopped to see the water. It was down over a high steep bank, too far to see fish effectively, so I grabbed my binoculars, and looking every bit the part of a tourist, began glassing the waters below. There was a distinct confluence line, made ever so much more visible by the strong foam line that it was holding. It was created at the top of a huge, long, straight pool where the water from the rapids surged in, forming a truly large reverse. Because the waters in the confluence line are turbulent, they are slower, and foam tends to pile up there. If foam piles up, food piles up, and fish pile up. As I watched with eagle's vision, sure enough, I could see black forms in the turbulence line.

We headed down over the bank. Nancy put a black Foam Beetle out into the foam line, and a head poked out and ate it. What followed was one of the last best days we ever had on the mighty river up in the Park. Shortly thereafter, lake trout were transplanted surreptitiously into Yellowstone Lake. The big lakers have all but eaten their way through the black-spotted cutthroats of Yellowstone Lake—the holding water for all the fish of the upper Yellowstone River, Pelican Creek, the Trident area, and others. Sadly, it does not look like I will be able to fish that wonderful confluence line again in my lifetime with the same success we enjoyed that day.

Nancy fishing the foam line where the in-rushing waters of the throat mix with the returning waters of the reverse. The reverse sweeps across in front of Nancy from left-to-right and rejoins the main currents near the rocks just visible behind her head.

Belly and Lip

I must confess that I find the belly of very deep straight pools the least interesting feature of them, unless there are feeding shallows along the sides or unless the edges are deep and perhaps overhung. Then that's the place I'm heading. The deep gut of the pool is a great place to hold big fish, and if there's an opportunity to fish anywhere along its edges, the fishing can be quite good. In Chapter One, I described my "Herculean" strength (and show-off rashness) that broke a test rod. I ended up fishing the waist-deep edge of a straight pool that was overhung with trees, brush, and grasses. The big fish were right there, tight to the edge and feeding on emerging midges. When hooked they shot to the deeper waters in the center of the pool. That made my job of fighting them every so much easier,

The tailout of a straight pool can often be of uniform depth from side to side. This means that the entire area can be a feeding zone. During hatches, one can find fish all over the tailout; this is also the zone for the night fisher. Big fish living in the belly of the pool back down into the tailout and feast during the dark hours.

In *Night Fishing for Trout,* L. James Bashline, describes the Goodsell pool on the Allegheny River at Coudersport, Pennsylvania, and says that for a century it was the greatest big trout producing pool in Pennsylvania, if not in the whole eastern U.S. He also added that, "The broad lip of slack water that formed the tail was the most perfectly created night fishing spot that I have ever seen." He then goes on to discuss the many big trout that anglers took in that tailout after dark.

Pay attention to the tailout of all pools, but especially those of big, straight pools. By the way, don't go looking for the Goodsell. In its zeal to channelize or dam every river in the U.S., the Army Corp of Engineers turned the Allegheny through Coudersport into a concrete sluice-way.

Below: The tailout of this pool on Montana's Armstrong Spring Creek is best fished from upstream to prevent having to cast up over the fast water of the riffle.

One year, Nancy and I were fishing in New Zealand and had found our way to a lovely stretch on a larger river. The two-track was certainly 4-wheelin' country, but we were equipped, and had worked our way into some particularly good-looking water.

As darkness crept up on us, the fish began to rise to a caddis hatch. We were working a riffle stretch at the time, and Nancy immediately took a nice 18-inch fish. Other trout were working, and I left her to have at them. I was headed upstream to the tailout of a long, straight pool above. Creeping up slowly, I saw a bulge in the water 40 to 50 away feet and in close to the rocky shore. It was a really nice fish, so I unloaded a cast.

As the 4-weight settled softly to the surface, a fish bolted our right in front of me, setting off a chain reaction that emptied the tailout of the pool. There were big wakes everywhere. It pays to take your time when fishing the tailout. Far better to go around and fish down into it, rather than casting up over it and spooking the whole thing.

The flat surface of the tailout can telegraph a fish's movements to an observant angler; the bulge I had noted in the story above, for example. In addition to a bulge, one may see a push of water as the fish swims along, or "nervous" water that somehow just doesn't fit in with what water in streams normally does. Pay especially close attention to such signals in all places where the water's surface is smoothly flowing.

Smoothly Curving Corner Pool

A smoothly curving pool on Alaska's Gibraltar. The outside corner is undercut and is lined with trees and debris piles.

There are probably more curving pools than straight ones, simply because the natural tendency for all flowing waters is to cut a side-to-side, curving channel. And classically, in smoothly curving pools, the outside edge is deep, and the inside edge is shallow. Typically, too, the current cuts against the outside of the pool creating undercut banks, sagging sod, falling and fallen trees, collapsing banks, flotsam washed in by high waters, and so on. Typically, too, if the water is over knee deep, all these features create prime lies, one after another all the way along the outside curve of the pool. Just like that debris washed in against the outside bank, the food coming down the river gets pushed right against that far bank. Where there's a concentration of currents, there's a concentration of food, there's a concentration of fish.

There are so many possibilities on the outside curve of such pools, that it would take a whole book just to cover them. Fortunately, it's not necessary to list every possibility to easily grasp the fact that the outside curve is an important stream feature that should be explored carefully and thoroughly. The fishing described on Alaska's Talachulitna in Chapter Two was mostly down the outside bank of long, smoothly curving corner pools.

Of course, there are pools in which the outside edge is not burrowing into a bank or undercutting the sod, and on which there are no trees or other growth. In New Zealand, for example, the rivers classically have three sections: (1) the high meadow valley section right up on the shoulder of the mountain, (2) the gorge section where the river cuts sharply down through the edge of the shoulder, and (3) the lowland section where the river runs out on the flat lands before dumping into the sea (or another river). When the snow melts in spring and/or heavy rains come, the rivers can, and do, roar. The amount of rock that spills out of the gorges is astounding, and the lower river sections typically look more like alluvial outwash than a simple stream. The channel changes often, and the broad rocky plain established by the river can change just as rapidly.

In such places, the curve of the river is simply flanked with rocks on both sides, although as is typical for any curve, the deep water is always on the outside of the curve. However, the deep water may not be up tight against the outside of the curve. There can be a shallow section that extends out a few feet before the bottom drops off sharply. It pays to watch such places very carefully because fish can slide up into the shallows to feed, and in a heartbeat be back in the deep water for protection.

The rocky banks of a curving pool on a New Zealand river.

In addition, many times fish will hold out in the deeper water, along the bottom in the many hydraulic slips set up behind the rocks. In other words, the whole corner can be a series of prime lies, and should be fished with care. I've found such places to be very favorable nymphing water.

On smoothly curving pools, there will be a reverse up at the top on the inside corner *(Figure 6.2)*. The size of the reverse will depend upon the size of the river and the speed of the inflowing current. Don't walk past this water. Many times, the reverse will be quite deep and contain a number of good fish. But even if there is no strong reverse, there very well can be a current edge, and it can be a good one. Anytime one encounters an "edge" or seam in the currents, it's our old friend the turbulence line, and it's a good spot. In fact, if one were to develop a real "eye" for seams and fish them exclusively, there would not be many days that one would go without fish.

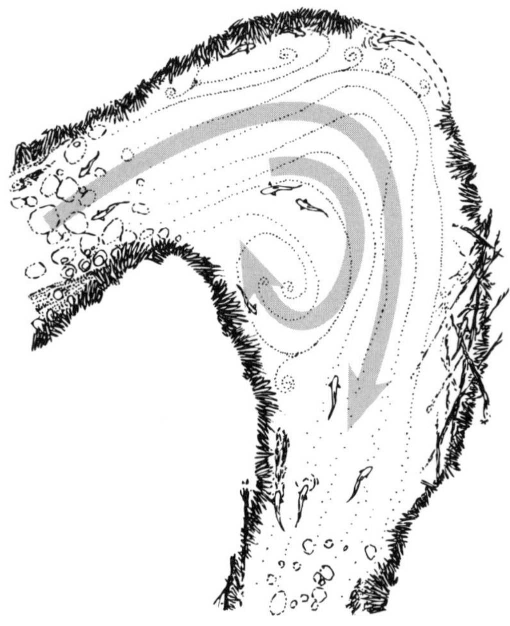

Figure 6.2. *Smoothly curving pools often have a reverse on the top, inside corner.*

Over the years, the water in the reverse will carve the bank back and form a spit of land that points directly into the turbulence line. Lenox Dick, writing in *The Art and Science of Fly Fishing*, calls such a place the "coffin corner" and says of it:

> "Here, if it is deep enough, there is a tremendous collection of food, and that is frequently where the big ones lie."

I will note that such places can be either feeding lies or prime lies, depending upon water depth.

Such "coffin corners" are frequent in all streams. What they represent is a concentration of currents, and as I've already said too many times, where currents concentrate, food concentrates, fish concentrate. On Henry's Fork, for example, there are clumps of sod, rocks, logs and other items in tight against the banks. As the current runs along the shore, it encounters these obstructions, and is forced out and around them. Thus, all the water from the shoreline to the outer edge of the obstruction is compressed at that outer edge as it flows around the object. All the food that drifts down between the shoreline and the outer edge of the object will also be forced out and around the obstruction. These are the feeding lies of the big boys, and they are the places that I really concentrate on when fishing the Fork.

One year Nancy and I were floating the Bighorn and doing quite well. It was early morning and the midge hatch was in full swing. I rowed and Nancy fished down the first long flat, taking several big browns. By the time we had drifted the fist mile, the sun was up and the clouds of midges started to burn off. We were coming into the top of a long, sweeping corner, and I pulled the boat over right at the top point of the

The coffin corner occurs at the very top end of a seam formed where the currents are concentrated by the bank, a big rock, or other such feature. Fish often hold in the "soft" water just at the top inside edge of the seam (the coffin corner) where I'm nymphing for salmon.

coffin corner. We had decided to grab a sandwich for breakfast, get something to drink, and perhaps wade and fish a bit. My rod was rigged with a sowbug and indicator, and I flipped it into the seam literally right beside the grounded drift boat. It was not a fishing cast. I was sitting on the gunwale and I simply wanted to get the rod pointed out of the boat, so that our clambering in and out didn't break it.

I didn't even get to set the rod down. The tip jerked around, and the line snapped tight. I was so startled that I didn't do anything. A mighty rainbow tore up out of the water, leaping as high as my head. I'm certain that I saw its fin up to its nose in an obscene gesture. It made an audible "smack" as it crashed to the water and tore off with my fly still firmly embedded in its jaw. Unfortunately, the line did not tear off after it. Turning quickly at the sound of the fish's re-entry impact, Nancy said, "What was that?"

"That was just me losing a huge rainbow," I mumbled weakly.

Why is it they always take the fly just when you're totally unprepared?

The tailout in smoothly curving pools is, as are all tailouts, a good place to watch for feeding fish. Like the main pool, they can be shallow on the inside and deep on the outside, or they may be more or less uniform in depth all the way across. And, as always, fish them with care.

Undercut Banks and Debris Piles

While I probably don't need to say anything about undercut banks, I'm going to. If the foam goes under there, food goes under there, and it's a prime lie. There are several examples of fishing undercuts on little streams in Chapter Three. Here, I'm dealing with streams that vary from the smallish side—15 to 30 feet across—to everything bigger. Never forgo an undercut if there's any possible way at all to get a fly in there. If the overhanging lip is high enough, there might be a chance to cast back under it. However, if it's too high above the surface, and water back under it is shallow, it will not be prime

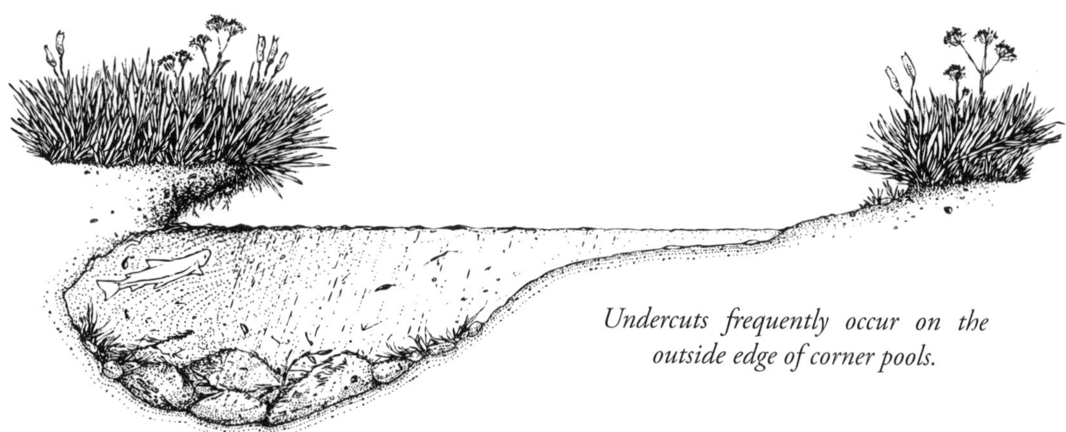

Undercuts frequently occur on the outside edge of corner pools.

water; a feeding area, yes. One should not be able to stand and look back into the dark recesses of a prime undercut.

So, mostly, I go for the across-stream approach with a strong upstream Reach Mend, or a direct down-and-across approach, getting the fly into the currents as close to the undercut as possible, and at a point where the currents are actually going into the undercut. Fish whatever you want/can back in such places. Give such places a shot if it's at all possible, they're great spots to find fish.

Debris piles can offer the same potential as undercuts. Although a pile of logs and other junk jammed against the bank may not be as undercut as an undercut, fish still have plenty of places to hold back among the debris. These places can be really tricky, however, because they have a way of snagging a fly like few other places on the stream. Still, it can be worth a try.

My old friend, Tom Roney, fishing a big curving pool on Michigan's Au Sable. The outside corner is filled with debris—a great chain of prime lies.

Fishing the "One Fly" contest in Jackson Hole one year, my team came in third after a rather trying day. I was impressed. We only needed one or two big fish to put us in the top slot. The first day I had fished a Gold Ribbed Hare's Ear into extinction and done quite well, so the second day, I decided to fish a big black Strip Leech and go for "meat." We were assigned to the main stem of the Snake, just north of Jackson Hole, and as we pulled into the boat launch, I noted that this stretch of water had lots of debris piles along the outside of the corners. Mentally, I shouted, "Oh, boy!"

At the first tangle of logs and sticks and roots, I flipped the leech into the sucking swirl of water at the upstream end of the pile and let it go down for a few seconds. On the strip, a very juicy 15-incher took it hard, and was summarily wrestled to the net, measured, and released. I knew that this was going to be a day to remember. And as it turned out, it was. At the second pile, I repeated the cast I'd made at the first one. The fly went down, and the line jerked tight. I jerked back. *I* was a jerk. I'd gotten the fly too close to the branches and was hooked up. Our guide heroically rowed the heavy drift boat back up the currents, but try as I might, I couldn't get the fly back. I even took off my shirt and reached as deep into the water as possible. In the end, I had to break the leader.

It's called the One Fly because that's all you're allowed for the day. My day was over as far as the contest was concerned, so I just fished out the day. It was great, but no cigar. Ah well, no guts, no glory, and no chance of becoming the goat, either.

Char Bar and Chum Bar

It was Jason's first Alaskan river. He was 15, and two months later would be driver's license age. This was his 16th birthday present a couple of months early. We'd chosen August so that we could fish for silvers. On the flight to Anchorage, Jason had issued a challenge, stating quite simply that he would catch more fish on the trip than I would. I gave him a bit of a hard time about it, but knew that I had my work cut out for me. This was going to be an intense fishing trip.

Although Jason had never fished Alaska, even at 15 he was a superb angler and didn't need any "help" to catch fish. And catch fish we did. We averaged over a hundred a day for each of us. That seems like a lot of fish, and it is, and it's my fault. Determined to give Jason a real "scrubbing," I had unwittingly opened the door to even greater competition. Smoothly curving pools, especially on larger waters, typically develop a shallow, often uniformly deep "bar" or "flat" in the lower half of the inside corner. If the currents slide over these with a nice even, yet noticeable flow, then there will be fish on them watching for food.

I knew this from having fished Alaska a number of times before, and so I immediately went to such a spot and started fishing with a fluorescent pink Gob-O-Eggs fly. The bar was loaded with arctic char and dollies, and they went absolutely gaga over the fly. It was literally a fish on every cast. I'd pulled a fast one on Jason, or so I thought, because it was strictly a numbers game. The bet was most fish, not biggest. Well, it only took Jason a couple of minutes to figure out that I was going to upstage him, and then he was standing on the next bar, with a Gob-O-Eggs securely lashed to his leader. After the first day, we called it a tie, and then decided to just see how many we could catch. So in the morning we'd hit the char bars then switch over to silvers and rainbows, then back to the char at evening, and finally onto the grayling rise right at dark. It was astounding fishing, all day long, every day long.

On smoothly curving pools such as this one on an Alaskan river, a char bar or chum bar can occur on the inside corner near the tailout.

Chum bars are no different than char bars, except they are usually much larger and can consist of sand as well as gravel. Alaska's big Alagnak offers one chum bar after another, The water is typically knee deep to waist deep, and flowing with enough strength to tug at the waders. Alaskan chums love magenta, and the chum bars are the perfect place to fish a big magenta leech with Brooks' Broadside Float. The smooth, even currents move the fly along while still holding it in a position at right angles to the flow, and one rarely needs to mend. At the end of the drift, I allow the fly to swing. While I get many fish on the swing—and usually more when the fly is deep—if the fish will come up, then I go with a magenta leech or flash fly dead drifted, *a la* Brooks, just under the film. The big fish come up and take the fly like a trout rising to a dry. There's just nothing like it. When the fish are still chrome bright, they take the leech with an eagerness that borders on lunacy, and fight as if possessed. I love chums.

Big char will take a fluorescent pink or orange Gob-O-Eggs with an eargerness that borders on insanity.

Sharp Corner Pool

Many times the course of the river's channel is dramatically altered, and the water is pointed off in a very much different direction than it was previously headed. The abrupt turning is caused by a high bank, a wall of stone, a rock slide, or other "immovable object." The result is a sharp corner pool. Gone is the gracious sweep of the water as it turns almost leisurely around the bend. Now it's bang and bump, grind and shove, as the water slams into the directional deflector. Such energy exertion causes the water to behave somewhat differently than in a smoothly curving pool.

One of the most noticeable effects is the production of a strong reverse on the outside of the current just where it slams into the deflector. This reverse can be big and deep, and during high flow periods can dig a rather impressive hole, both impressively deep and impressively large. In lower flow periods, the reverse itself will be smaller. The part of the hole dug during high water that is furthest from the current will form a slough or back water, known affectionately among anglers as "frog water." Well, there can most certainly be other things in there besides frogs—like trout in cold water streams, and other species in warmer waters. I guess I've said it so often that it's getting monotonous, but I'll say it again: don't rush the water. Pay attention to anyplace that can potentially hold feeding fish.

This reverse on the outside of the corner, right where the water splashes against the immovable object, is one very good place to find fish. And if it's got any depth to it at all, it will be a prime lie. Fish will also cruise out of this prime area into the back-water area.

A sharp corner pool on Montana's Rock Creek. Jason took many trout from the deep water against the rock face.

One time in New Zealand, I was fishing up a rather large river system. The water coursed along between high rock walls, and then opened into pasture land. Because of the river's size, there are usually a fair number of fish in it, and sometimes a few bigger ones (in the 28- to 30-inch class), which is what I was hoping for. I came to a spot where the going got seriously tough and I decided to stop and head back. Then I heard a rise. I knew it couldn't be that far away, but I hadn't seen it. Just there, the river struck the face of a cliff, not in a hard push, but more of a gently slide. The water upcurrent from the cliff was fairly deep and slid along as deep water does, without the ripping and tearing of a riffle or rapids. I listened. There it was again. Now I thought that I knew where it was coming from, but I could still see nothing.

I climbed the very steep bank, holding bushes and tree branches to help with the ascent. At the top, I was confronted with the famed New Zealand "bush," a nearly impenetrable mixture of fallen trees, brush, and forest all tossed into a slurry that defies description, and defies passage. But, a fish was calling, and so I pressed on. When I figured I was on the other side of the current, I climbed out on a tree overhanging the water and searched the surface, about 20 feet below. There it was, feeding in the reverse on the outside of the corner. Crawling back down the trunk to the bank, I continued on around and came out above the big, slow reverse. The rainbow took the dry on the first drift. It was 25-inches long, and in excellent condition. It was worth the scramble over the river and through the woods.

Once, when Jason and I were floating Canada's Bow River, Jason found a relatively small, but very deep reverse in a sharp corner pool. He climbed high up on the steep bank above the river and looked down. The reverse was jammed with big trout. He started after them immediately. I came drifting down in another boat a few minutes later, and he called for me to come over. The reverse was foam-covered and black with depth. The fish would take a deeply presented Hare's Ear or other nymph, and we had a fantastic hour or so at the spot.

At one point, the action slowed a bit, and I tossed my nymph upstream further than normal, so that it would sweep into the turbulence line between the reverse and main current. The indicator went under and I set the hook. Nothing. I thought I'd caught a branch sunken deep in the reverse, so I gave a couple of jerks on the line. Then *it* flashed deep in the currents and both Jason and I sucked in our breaths—it was big, as in *really* big. And off it went in the currents, pulling line off the reel with determined ease. I ran downriver, but soon came to a place where it was either stop or swim. I stopped. The fish did not, and the backing was getting close to the bitter end. I put pressure on the fish, and as it turned and came back up a bit, I reeled hard. "Maybe, just maybe," I thought. Then there was a sudden surge, and the 3X parted cleanly. Yes, there can be really big fish in those outside-corner reverses.

Typically, in these sharp corner pools, the water downstream of the corner is deepest against the outside, where the currents tear off in their new direction. But there can be a really deep reverse on the inside corner, too. There's probably more variability in these sharp corner pools than in other pool types, because there can be such variability in current speeds entering the pool, and because there is so much variation in high water flows. A river that undergoes powerful high water periods in the spring will often have very deep, sharp corner pools.

Because there is such variability in depths, fishing any pool is not a cut-and-dried event. There are usually prime areas along the outside of the currents and feeding areas on the inside, but, add to the currents such things a undercuts, heavy vegetation growth, debris piles, and in-stream boulders, rock ledges, and so on, and one has a veritable plethora of variables. The best thing to do is use one's understanding of sheltering lies, feeding lies, and prime lies and read, read, read. And don't forget the tailout. Always suspect that fish will be back there looking for food.

Also don't forget that stream size will have a strong effect on fish positions. Dave Graebel had graciously invited me to fish his King Creek Ranch in Colorado a number of times, but other engagements had blocked my way. This time, though, Nancy and I had a clear spot on the calendar, and we loaded our motor home in preparation for the trip west. We arrived in late evening to the possible prospect of rain on the morrow.

The next morning as Dave and I rigged our rods, Nancy and Dave's wife, Linda, drove off for other pursuits, leaving us to "suss out" the trout under an overcast sky. Everything was pointing to a great morning's fishing: the air was warm, the clouds threatened rain but couldn't make good on it, and the air was alive with midges. Sure enough, the fish were actively feeding when we entered the water just above the canyon.

"We'll fish up to the wooden bridge," Dave told me, "And we'll get picked up at 12:30 for lunch."

The distance was perhaps a third of a mile, and having never fished this water, all I could offer was "Okay."

Ha! Fish up to the wooden bridge? We only covered three sharp corner pools before it was time to hike all the way up to the bridge. The fish practically threw themselves on our flies. Dave loves the dry fly, although he is not adverse to fishing nymphs, buggers, or other such fare. It was his morning. Fish were rising everywhere along the length of the pools, and I spotted while Dave cast. While he played his fish, I'd toss a hopper and dropper up into the pool and take a fish on the dropped Bead Head Prince Nymph, and occasionally on the hopper.

The inside corner at the top of the sharp corner pools was especially productive, but we took fish from every pool part. We'd stand well below the tailout and fish it first. Then we'd move up and get into a pile of fish in the belly, finishing by casting long into the inside corner and to the lip at the head. It was a truly spectacular morning.

Dave Graebel playing one of many that took the fly at the tailout of the pools.

Island Pools and Back Channels

Islands in a river can form two curving pools, and typically there can be a gravel bar extending upstream from the top of the island that offers great feeding lies. But there are all sorts of variations. For example, some islands form smaller back channels, leaving the main channel without any noticeable decrease in flow. Those back channels can be red hot, though. When the water is running high enough to feed the back channels with a good flow, they will hold many big trout.

Nancy and I were fishing the Bighorn one August and pulled into a small back channel. I beached the boat at the top of the channel because I didn't want to run over any fish that might be in there. The top of the narrow watercourse, just where it left the main river, didn't look like much. It was overhung with bushes and appeared only a few feet wide. Downstream it opened into a smoothly curving pool about thirty feet wide. I pitched the nymph as tight to the overhanging brush as possible and was rewarded with an immediate stop of the indicator. Thinking I'd caught an underwater branch, I jerked back hard. A huge brown jumped right up into the brush and broke me off instantly.

When something like this happens, get back at it as fast as humanly possible, even if your hands are shaking. In a few moments, a new fly was plopping down in the same spot and the indicator shot under once again. This time my strike was down and across to pull the fish's head around so it wouldn't jump into the brush. It jumped clear. A few minutes later, and I netted 24 inches of brown trout.

Nancy took the rod and I took the camera. On her very first cast, she also hooked and subsequently landed 24 inches of brown trout. We knew something special was happening and so we kept at them, trading the rod and the camera. When we got to fish number 12, we stopped. It was "only" 19 inches, the first one under 20 that we'd caught.

The first fish in the net was two feet of very healthy brown trout.

We were into the "small" fish, and it was time to move on (when you move on from 19-inch browns, you know that you've had a *very* special day, indeed).

Plunge Pool

Growing up in northwestern Pennsylvania, the Little Sandy held my particular attention—especially once I could drive. A stretch from the pump house at the Polk State Institution to the highway bridge on Pennsylvania route 62 was fly-fishing only. My friends and I pounded the place mercilessly, but there were two spots that really held our attention: the Pump-House Pool and the Trestle Pool. Both of them were plunge pools; deep, mysterious, and nearly impossible to catch anything from, except little guys.

At the time, we fished those pools like everyone else. We'd wade up to the lower end and toss our flies up to the falling water, allowing them to drift back down to us. At the time, we didn't understand the folly of it; that's the way all the anglers pictured on calendars did it. What did we know? As it turns out, this approach is totally wrong. The fly lands up on the white water just below the plunge. This water is white because it's filled with air bubbles rushing back to the surface after being sucked down by the plunging water. If the air is going up, it's taking the water with it. This spot is one of upwelling currents. No streamer or wet fly or nymph will sink in such a place without a lot of shot on it, which at the time we weren't using because we'd been scolded by an elder fly fisher a year or so earlier—"*Real* fly fishers don't use shot," he growled at us.

In addition, standing at the bottom of the pool and casting up is basically standing at the tailout and casting up over it into the belly of the pool. Any fish in the tailout will spook and rip upstream to hide in the bottom of the plunge pool. So, for the entire time I lived in Pennsylvania, I fished those pools incorrectly.

Nancy and I moved to Wisconsin in 1968, and went back to Pennsylvania to visit family several times a year. On one such trip, I stopped at a shop in Ohio and bought an R.H. Woods cane rod. It was 7' 9" with a staggered ferrule. This was in the days before graphite, and I was slowly making the graduation from my glass rods to cane. It was the perfect rod for the Little Sandy.

I got to the Pump-House Pool just in time to see a mayfly dun flit off the edge of the low-head dam and duck into the bushes. A quick check showed that the *Isonychia* mayflies were hatching. The nymphs are strong swimmers and head to shore like little minnows. They crawl out, and the adults emerge on a rock or log (or concrete wall, in this instance). Quickly knotting on a Red Brown Nymph, I began to wade into the usual and customary spot, when I had an idea. Whether it was a mental note floating around somewhere aimlessly that just happened to settle out at that moment or not, I don't know. But it was shades of the culvert pool on Shell Creek and many others that I had fished since that day.

I went on across the stream and came in right on the downstream edge of the dam. I was partially hidden by trees and undergrowth to my rear, and I had just enough room to make a roll cast. It unrolled right into the plunging water. The floating line, leader, and nymph shot to the bottom in a heartbeat, and I gave the line a short strip to swim the fly. Immediately I was fast to a 15-inch brown, certainly the biggest I'd ever taken out of that pool, and certainly one of the holdover fish. I took a few more out of the pool the same way, all smaller, but all nice fish for that little stream.

The trestle pool on the Little Sandy.

Downstream of the Pump-House Pool was the Trestle Pool, a much larger hole with a six-foot high dam. There were big browns in there, and this looked like my morning to finally get one. I headed cross-country, past other pools that I should have fished, but I was eager to stay with the hatch and try my new found tactic in the trestle plunge.

My trophy horned chub.

The cast hadn't even settled when the line jerked hard. I reefed back and promptly landed the biggest horned chub that I'd ever caught—10 inches long, with a crimson belly and prominent "horns" all over the top of its head and nose.

I've fished plenty of other plunge pools over the years and always found them most-hospitable to a fly presented in the plunge.

Confluence Pool

Often, where a tributary enters a larger stream, there will be a pool. It's unique in that it is a mixing pot of currents. Depending upon the size and speed of the tributary, the pool may be small to large, and the mixing may be hardly noticeable or it may be rather strong, with many confused currents. Typically there will be a "seam," or "turbulence line," "foam line," or "confluence line" *(Figure 6.4).* This zone of mixing water is an especially good place to find feeding fish because it concentrates food. This is the type of pool on the Missouri where Jason took the big brown in the story in Chapter One.

Figure 6.4. *A confluence pool where Cabin Creek enters the Madison. Note crescent-shaped foam line where the currents intersect.*

Reading Rapids

So what's the difference between a riffle and a rapids? Well, the names sort of say it, don't they? In a riffle, the moderately flowing water jingles down over stones creating standing waves. A rock or two shows here and there, perhaps. Maybe a gravel bar appears in low-water conditions. But a rapids? Well, first of all the water is ***rapid***. The bottom is inclined enough so that the water literally rips—rips the fine particles and even the smaller stones out of the bottom, leaving rocks and boulders. Perhaps more than anything, boulders, or certainly very large rocks, characterize rapids. Rapids are a place of extremes—extremes in water depth, extremes in bottom erosion, extremes even in current speeds, as we shall see. Rapids are always places to be searched carefully by the fly fisher—carefully in terms of wading, and carefully in terms of making certain that no good water goes unexplored.

The Secret River

I can think of no better example of rapids than Montana's Madison. Certainly there are rivers like the Deschutes with more powerful and formidable looking rapids, certainly there are streams like Colorado's Roaring Fork that have as many rapids, certainly there are streams like Wyoming's Green River that pour through rock and boulder country with all the zeal of the Madison, but on a mile-per-mile basis, the Madison is a perfect example of everything that rapids can offer to the fly fisher. From the day I first set foot in the Madison in 1962, it has been a particular love of mine.

The Madison starts at the famous confluence pool at Madison Junction in west central Yellowstone Park. Here the waters of the Firehole and Gibbon co-mingle to form the Madison. At its origins, it's a meadow stream, and not a small one either. It pours with vigor through Elk Meadows and then into a series of long riffles and several nice pools, with a few hints of rapids before entering Hebgen Lake, just outside West Yellowstone, Montana. This upper section can offer some good fishing, and I go there from time to time just to see it and fish some of its storied holes and flats.

Leaving Hebgen, the Madison immediately plunges into rapid waters, tearing around the bend, down a straight away, into another deep, sharp bend pool, and onward before it dives into Quake Lake. This section between Hebgen and Quake can offer some outstanding fishing at times, and when the times are right, it's a fun place to be. During the hatch of the Salmon Fly (*Pteronarcys californica*) is one of those times. The big stoneflies lumber clumsily through the air, and are often tossed onto the water by canyon winds. In addition, when the females are egg-laying, there can be many flies, both in the air and on the water. The fish do not hesitate to eat the big adults. They may hesitate to eat the *angler's* fly, though, and that's where this discussion is going.

Figure 7.1. *Look carefully to find the secret river all the way along the shoreline (dashed line).*

Rapids are tough places to put a fly down and expect it to float with any sort of dead drift. But there are some tricks to it. First comes reading waters, then comes the fishing. In all rapids, there is a "secret river" *(Figure 7.1)*. It may be quite narrow, and then again it may be fairly wide. It's the easy water, the place one can toss a fly without much need to do more than use a Harvey-style leader to get a good float. During the Salmon Fly hatch (and every other hatch for that matter), the fishing can be fast and furious in the secret river, and it's the first place I hit. It's the water right against the bank—you know, that stuff one wades through to get out there into the "real" river. But think about it for a moment: Where's the best place for an energy-conserving trout to park itself while getting food in the easiest fashion? That's right: In the slow water next to shore where the stoneflies are hanging on every bush like overly ripe fruit.

When guiding anglers on the Madison, my long-time friend, Mike Lawson, tells clients to cast into all those places where one wouldn't normally fish—in other words, the secret river. Those that pay attention to his advice find out very quickly that Mike is a shrewd water-reader, indeed. Most anglers use the secret river as their wading lane, when in fact, it should be their fishing lane.

The secret river on Russia's Sidorovka.

So, lesson number one in reading rapids is very simple—find the secret river on either side of the rapids, and fish it hard. Some of it will be deep and some of it will be shallow, so expect to find a mixture of prime lies and feeding lies. Some of it may have undercut banks and sometimes there are boulders blocking your wading; too deep on the outside to go around and too tall to clamber over. One has to haul out and walk around. But when you do, watch it! The hydraulic cushion right in front of that boulder may be holding a boulder-sized brown. Don't race through the secret river!

One year, Jason and I had gone to fish the stretch between Hebgen and Quake lakes during the Salmon Fly emergence and egg-lying period. The bugs were there, and we were confident that we'd find the fish. There are a couple of places that one can cross from the dirt track that borders the west side—if you know exactly where they are, and

Below: The section of the Madison between Hebgen and Quake lakes where Jason and I fished the secret river along the far bank.

if you are a bold wader. Being with another person is a good idea. We linked arms and marched across. Once on the other side, Jason went down so he could fish back up, and I went up to fish even further up.

I hopped into the secret river, and almost immediately began taking fish. They were in tight in most places because the secret river was narrow in much of that section. I knew that, and fished the fly up with a Puddle Mend, sometimes literally a few inches from the shoreline. Fish would occasionally come out of the deeper water, a foot or two out, and pick off the imitation only a few inches from shore. It was one of those days that sticks in the memory banks for a lifetime.

As I fished up, a couple of other anglers showed up and watched me land one, cast and hook another. They dove into the river and waded out as far as possible and cast as far a possible. I don't have to tell you the total number of fish they caught. I just kept picking them off, and that only got the other guys pounding harder. But fishing fishless water is never successful, no matter how hard one applies every trick in the book. I felt bad for them, but there wasn't really anything I could do at that point in time, except catch more fish, so I did.

Interestingly, the secret river is not a secret at all to one select group of individuals. In fact, it is their preferred area to fish. This set of individuals are the float guides. Their mantra, repeated time and time again to clients who struggle to comply, is: "Get the fly closer to the bank."

Odd isn't it? The guys floating mid-river are told by their guides to pound the banks, while the guys that are wading struggle to get their flies to mid-river.

In the early/mid 1980s, I appeared in three videos from 3M/Scientific Anglers. One of them was *Fly Fishing for Trout*. It included introductory information on dries, nymphs, and streamers. All the fish were to be "live" catches, no smoke-and-mirrors. This was the beginning of video fly-fishing instruction, and it was all shot in film, and edited in film—a very costly and time-intensive process. There was no digital editing, no HD video. It was 16mm film with the final print converted to 1-inch video for duplication. What it meant to me was the need to catch fish on command. Believe me, it's not something that I was used to doing, and didn't feel totally confident I could do. But I was willing to give it everything I had.

We wanted to film some deep-nymphing tactics on the Madison just upstream from Three-Dollar Bridge. The reason was simple; the water looks great there and the scenery, shooting upstream, is stunning. It is classic-looking trout water that begs to be waded, but setting the camera up in the currents was a difficult task. The tripod had to be anchored with weights and the shooting angle had to be correct. I told the camera crew where I would be fishing, and told them to keep out of that area as they moved back and forth from the shore while attempting to get the camera steady. I also told the rest of the crew to stay away from the water—at least 50 feet away. I did not want even the slightest chance that the fish might see them moving around.

Now, please understand: A film crew is essential, but there's a lot of down time for some members while others are doing their necessary prep work. The sound crew had nothing to do while the cameraman steadied the tripod. The director was wandering around, twiddling his thumbs—he'd even go off and fish sometimes. In those blank times, there was a lot of talking, wandering around, and just general fussing. It's really easy to upset the water if such down times are allowed to become free-for-alls. But, everyone was a fly fisher, and understood the need to keep the water clean. The entire project depended on it.

Once the camera was in place, the director jumped into action, telling me how to wade up the section, what I needed to remember to say, where to fight the fish, and so on. All this while the sound guy was making certain that the gaffer's tape holding the hidden mic against my chest was on tight enough so that when it was removed it would rip off a few unneeded hairs. During the set up, I was standing in the river at the bottom of the filming beat, watching the water in a bit of a nervous state. I really had to catch something, no messing around, no fishing through without a bump. As I stood there, I saw a caddis pupa husk drift by. By the time the director was ready to make the call of "Action," there were more husks in the drift, and so I tied on a soft-hackled pupal imitation. My selecting the fly and tying it on was to be filmed, which was why I hadn't done it previously.

Turning my back to the camera, I began to fish. The stretch of water was classic rapids: big boulders, racing, heavy current tongues, big standing waves, and lots of gurgling, splashing water sound. It looked and sounded great. And where did I fish? About three feet out from the shore in the waist-deep water of the secret river. There were a couple of big boulders upstream about 20 feet, and the current tongues on the outside were perfect "coffin corners" (see Chapter Six). I made only about three casts—just enough I told them afterward, so they could get the framing and focus perfect—and the indicator rocketed under. It was a nice 17-inch rainbow that did all the things that rainbows are supposed to do. We got great shots of jumps, grey-hounding, hard runs, and a splashy netting. I even got most of my lines right the first or second time. Thank you, secret river, I felt like a king!

Then, because I had done well, the director decided that we needed a long shot off the bridge, shooting downstream as I fished up into the camera. So, the big boredom again. Everyone hustled around resetting the cameras, relocating the sound EQ, and in general trying to look busy. Me? I had already picked out the water I wanted to protect, and was vigilantly guarding it. It was another stretch of the secret river that consisted of a long, rather narrow gravel bar right in against the shoreline. The outside edge dropped off into a dark fast current, and I knew there would be fish on the outside of that bar.

Finally, everything was in place. It's always been interesting to me how a camera crew can pull people in like flies to honey or moths to a flame. By the time the camera was set and weighted, the sound guy had me clearly in ear, and the director had told me how I was supposed to catch the fish and then fight it (yes, really), there were about 50 people on the bridge. Many were fishermen, but others just looked liked tourists.

The director was up on the bridge and had already instructed the crowd to be silent when he yelled "Action." At his shout, I swung into action, and again, only about three casts into the thing, the indicator went under. I lifted the rod tip, and felt some serious weight. Off the fish went like a house afire, tearing off great, ragged lengths of line as it threaded its way upcurrent from boulder to boulder. This was what we'd come for. The rod tip whipped wildly, I ran and splashed water, pulling and accentuating my movements, playing to the camera. Everyone on the bridge watched intently.

The big fish swung wide and then headed down. I had to stand and fight because the camera had me chained to that spot. The fish fought deep and hard, and I—and everyone else, I'm guessing—assumed it was a big brown. Finally it got close enough to see in the deep water. It flashed silver—a big rainbow. Now I was getting really excited. I got my net ready, and drawing the fish around and headfirst down stream, I shoved the net deep and came up with an absolutely huge…whitefish. Nearly 24 inches long and heavy in the body, I lifted it high for the camera, and then dipped the net back into the water.

A whitefish? Yes, and a really nice one, too!

The crowd went crazy, whistling, shouting and in general, cheering. Little did they know.

Then I said to the sound guy, over my mic, "It's a huge whitefish." He relayed it to the cameraman in a loud shout. Suddenly the bridge crowd went silent. It was as if they were all thinking, "Whitefish? It's just a *whitefish?!*" Then, they all drifted away, leaving the bridge empty. I thought it was a really solid piece of fishing, and the whitefish was certainly of trophy size. But, my shining crown quickly came sliding down around my ankles, and I had to be very careful not to trip and fall headfirst into the secret river.

The Secret Pools (a.k.a. Pockets)

Every rapids is filled with secret pools. They lie just downstream of the boulders that give rapids their character *(Figure 7.2)*. Each pool is bounded by a fast current tongue on each side, and its belly is made of two reverse currents flowing up against the backside of the boulder. In reverse of the usual arrangement; these pools are deep at their edges and shallower in the middle. Where the two tongues converge downstream, there's a nice turbulence line. Occasionally, a boulder is pressed in tight against the shore. Its pool will have only one current tongue on the outside and only one reverse. These spots can even be deeper than some of the mid-stream secret pools. No matter, these are still real pools.

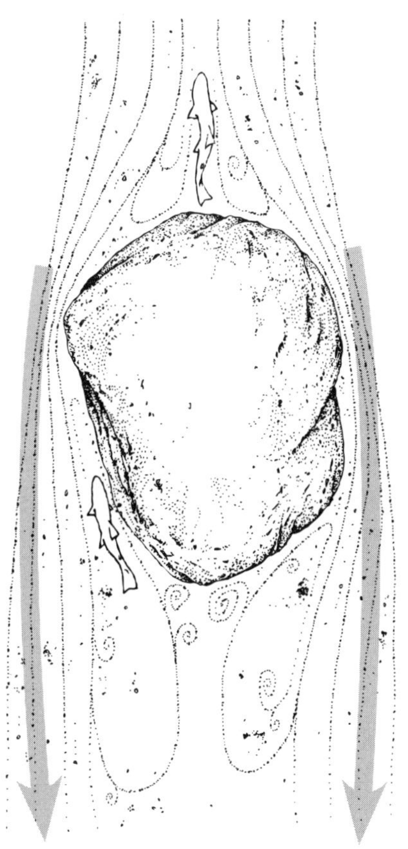

***Figure* 7.2.** *The secret pools found behind boulders are micro versions of their larger namesakes.*

In fishing lingo, we call these secret pools, "pockets," and as we've noted earlier, they, like the boulders that form them, are characteristic of rapids. Fish like to hang out in pockets. There's everything they need: current tongues to bring in a constant stream of food, slow water to park in, a big boulder to hide under, and on big water like the Madison, a seemingly impossible place to get a fly into, dead-drift. The trick is to fish up-current into the pockets, using an "overpowered" Tuck Cast/Mend or Pile Cast/Mend.

As you can see, I prefer to use two different names for this skill, depending on what I'm trying to accomplish. With a nymph, the cast or mend is a Tuck, and with a dry fly, it's a Pile. I find that the name change helps to differentiate the application (nymph or dry), as well as the end result: one version causes a strong "tucking" of the nymph downward, the other, due to the air resistance of the dry fly and leader, causes a deliberate pile of slack on the surface. Either way, the overall idea is fairly straightforward, but the execution does require some practice.

Many of the boulders in a rapids have secret pools where fish can find all three types of lies.

The way I make the Tuck or Pile is quite different than the original. The original was made by "checking" the cast so that the line recoiled a bit, dropping the nymph to the water with slack in the leader. The way I make the Tuck/Pile Cast should already be familiar territory for those anglers used to making an "Overpowered Curve Cast" to get a fly to hook to the left or right. Basically the Tuck/Pile Cast is a horizonally oriented curve tipped to the vertical. The Overpowered Curve is made by stopping the rod hard (really almost a "bounce" of the rod) so that the tip flexes very deeply, with the ultimate result being a strong curve in the line *(Figure 7.3)*. When done in the vertical position, the line is aimed high, like making a false cast, so that the curve has the necessary space in which to form over-and-down. Lifting the rod hand up and forward into the direction of the cast, immediately after the curve has formed, can help create an even more effective presentation (indeed, line can even be shot into the curve by shooting and lifting simultaneously). The end result, when done right (yes, it requires practice), is either the nymph or the end of the line aiming strongly downward.

To make the mend variation of this general Tuck/Pile skill, make a straight cast, again, aimed high like a false cast, and immediately after stopping the rod at the end of the forward stroke, make a short, quick, up-down movement with the rod tip. This will introduce a curve similar to the overpowered cast; hold the rod high so that the curve has room to form over and down. A weighted nymph will flip over and pull the line after itself—the Tuck. A dry will lag back and cause the leader to fall in a heap just off the end of the line—the Pile.

I was fishing the Madison one day with a couple of friends, and they dropped me off in an area of heavy riffles. I fished down the water without so much as a sniff from the fish. Downstream, the bottom pitched a bit more and clearly could be classified as rapids. I needed to get to the other side, so I headed down-and-across. The riffles were a bit more than I had anticipated at that point—they were more like a run (see Chapter Eight). I was moving faster than I liked, and anticipated a potential swim. I had no wading staff, but I had my rod and a little trick to go along with it.

This trick has saved my butt more times than I care to admit. I learned this from Joe Brooks' book, *Trout Fishing*. The idea is to plop the rod into the water, *parallel to the surface and straight across the currents*. Be careful and don't allow the tip to head into the bottom. Keep the entire rod just under and parallel to the surface. Hold it firmly in this position a few inches under the surface. The strong pressure of the fast water against the length of the rod gives you instant stability and control.

Using that trick I made it to the other side and went down to where the other two were fishing. They looked startled and asked, "You waded across?" They looked at each other and shrugged. I went fishing.

There was a rock that I wanted to have a shot at, so I worked down-and-across until I intersected the turbulence line about 40 feet below the broad, low boulder. I moved up a bit and tossed my nymph and indicator right up to the very back of the boulder, using a Tuck Cast. The indicator didn't even settle, it just went right under. I set the hook, and a 19-inch rainbow shot into the air. Almost to hand, the hook popped out and the fish slid back into the currents. It had been well worth the fearful wade.

But that's not the only rainbow that I've picked up behind a boulder. On a different day, and several thousands miles away on Alaska's Moraine, Ray Beadle and I headed downstream after the fierce fishing experience described in Chapter Six. As we waded into the top of the next pool, I looked back and up through the rapids we'd walked around, and knew I'd have to go back. The big rainbows were in the top of the pool,

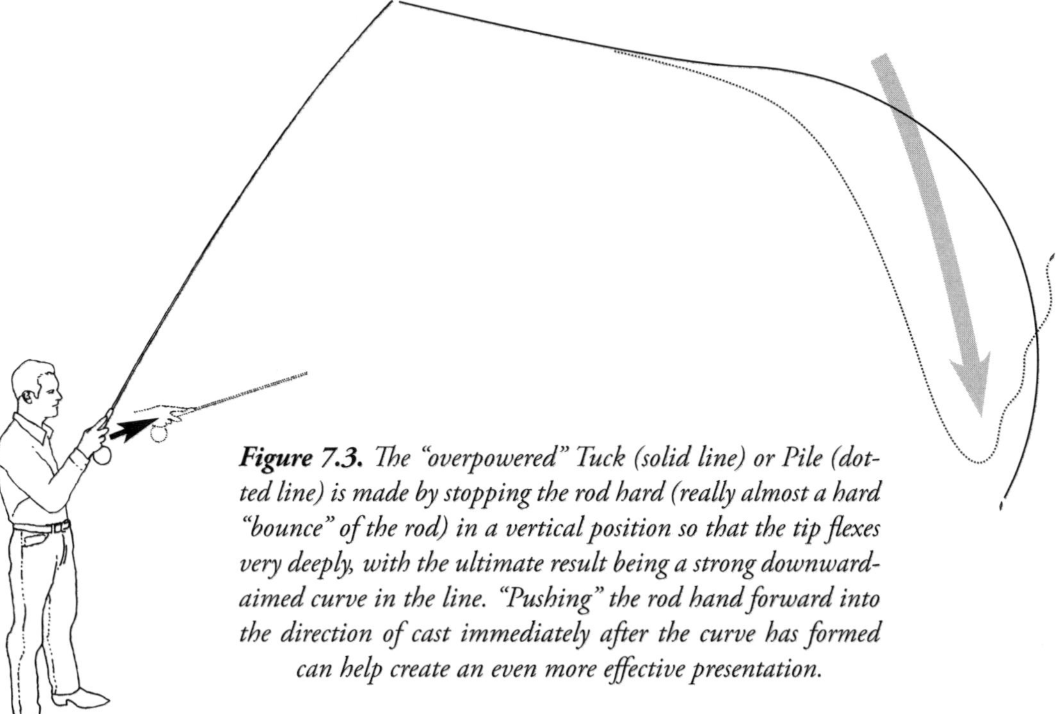

Figure 7.3. *The "overpowered" Tuck (solid line) or Pile (dotted line) is made by stopping the rod hard (really almost a hard "bounce" of the rod) in a vertical position so that the tip flexes very deeply, with the ultimate result being a strong downward-aimed curve in the line. "Pushing" the rod hand forward into the direction of cast immediately after the curve has formed can help create an even more effective presentation.*

but I knew they'd be in the rapids, too, and I wanted to pry them out. As I waded in at the lower end, I heard loud splashing, like someone running in shallow water. I turned and looked to my right. Here came a big brown bear, running full tilt through a shallow back channel, straight at me and less than a hundred feet away. I waded into the rapids *right now* without regard to a possible swim. Suddenly the bear dove into the water feet first and came up with a big sockeye, turned, and hauled it up into the bushes to eat.

With my adrenaline peaking, I fished the rapids like a wild man. The secret pool behind every boulder held a big rainbow. The majority jumped off or otherwise escaped from the barbless hook because I had to play them hard. There was no wading after them in the rapids, and they were too big to just haul in. But, what a ride—scared to death by a big Alaskan brown bear and brought back to life by big Alaskan rainbows.

There were big rainbows like this one behind nearly every big boulder in the "brown bear" rapids.

There are times when one might have the opportunity to fish into boulder pockets from an across-stream position. The great difficulty here comes with the fast current tongues set up on either side of the boulder. Again, a Tuck/Pile Cast/Mend is a great way to get the fly in there and keep it there long enough for the fish to take it. Fishing the current tongues from an across-stream position is more easily done than fishing the pocket. I love to nymph these seams, pitching the fly up into the very top of a seam and allowing the fly to run right down the current tongue. One can hold the rod high and control the pathway of the fly very well. When I need to reach out a bit further than the rod will go, I Reach Mend upstream very strongly so the line is aimed more down and across, rather than just across. This gives me controllable slack that I can then flip back upstream as needed to control the drift.

Sometimes, one can fish down into the pockets, too. One time, Jason and I were fishing an Arctic river, hunting for sea-run browns. We had entered the river's canyon stretch, which was literally miles of heavy rapids with an occasional deep pool. Suddenly we came to a stretch that held some Atlantic salmon—late season fish that made up the last run of Atlantics for the year. Our good friend, Jim Hagar, had located a fish that was holding in a current tongue about 20 feet below a boulder and on its far side. Deciding to approach from above, Jason cast right over the top of the boulder. The fly plopped in and immediately began swinging down and across. The boulder held the line, allowing the fly to swing into the tongue on the far side of the pocket and hang there. A few moments later, the salmon rolled up and inhaled the white Marabou Muddler.

When fishing from a drift boat, spend some time "picking the pockets" in rapids. But watch, if the secret river along the bank is deep and characterized by undercuts, overhanging brush, boulders in tight to the bank, and so on, then chances are the bigger fish will be there.

Reverse Currents

It seems odd to think about reverse currents in a discussion of rapids, but they are there. First, there are the soft reverses behind every boulder, as mentioned earlier. That's why it's so necessary to use a cast or mend that will pile the leader into the pocket, and why I like to fish up into them. A Puddle Cast/Mend won't work because the line lands first, right in front of the rod tip. By the time the fly gets to the water, the line has been whipped downstream by the fast currents, and drag sets in, pronto.

But there are often other reverses. Remember, these rotating foam/food/fish concentrators form anyplace where there are differential current pressures. Reverses often set up on the upstream side of boulders that sit against the bank. Currents striking the front of the rock push out to the sides. When it strikes the bank, it rotates back upstream, forming the reverse. I love to fish down into these. The fly drifts in and then just goes with the flow. I'll often revert to the small-stream tactic of allowing the fly to run down and into the reverse and then pulling it back up.

There are also places where debris piles up along the shoreline, against a big boulder, on the point of a gravel bar or island, and so on. These are always spots that need some serious attention. One day I was fishing the Madison with my long-time, late friend, Jim Greenlee. His home was just upstream from the Raynolds Pass Bridge and on the south side of the river. It was a day when we thought the PMDs would be hatching, but they were not. It was time to go down and dirty.

I tied on two big, brown, Down and Dirty Leeches, clamped a split-shot above each fly, and began pounding for big fish. At first I worked the pockets, but they didn't give up much, so I started to focus on every other possible spot that I thought might hold fish. Most of the trout came from the debris piles and regions of undercut banks in the secret river. Another angler had been watching me, and he called across stream the single most asked question, "What fly are you using?"

"A size 10 Adams," I yelled.

"Not with a splash like that," he called back.

I cast the flies across so he could see what I had on, and how they were rigged. He caught the line, looked in disbelief at the big flies and shot, and shook his head. But when he dropped the flies back into the water, I noticed he was digging a fly box out of his vest.

Remember the story from Chapter One about my being spooled on the Newhalen in Alaska? Well, I wouldn't even classify that water as rapids, it was so powerful and so awesome that it reminds me of the huge water one sees in places like the Grand Canyon. Just stunning. So we'll call it a "super-rapids." From where those super-rapids tear out of the Newhalen's canyon, there's still a half-mile of "regular" rapids downstream. But just where they come tearing out, the walls of the canyon fall back a couple of hundred feet on either side. That's where the giant reverses were set up. Reverses can set up in any rapids, anywhere there's anything that can create a current pressure differential.

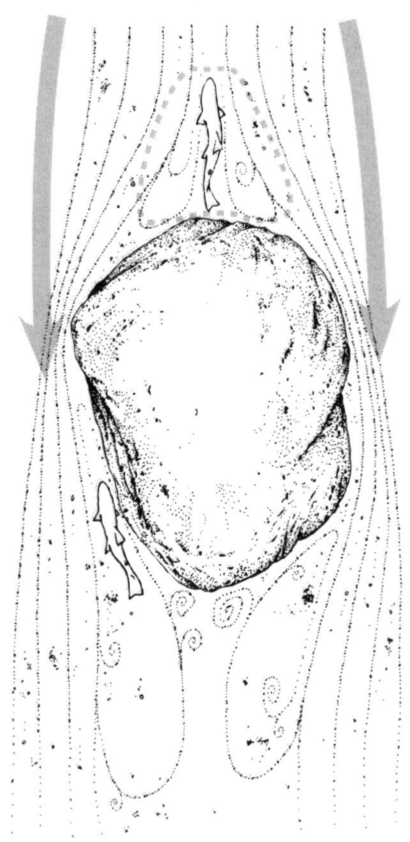

***Figure** 7.4. Does this illustration look familiar? In addition to the secret pool, make sure you pay keen attention to the hydraulic cushion in front of boulders.*

Hydraulic Cushions

Rapids are also the place of the hydraulic cushion. This phenomenon occurs at the upstream edge (face) of boulders. One look, and it's obvious. The water on the upstream side is higher than the water on the downstream side. The current striking the face of the boulder is forced up, down, and out to the sides. There is also rebound—water hitting the rock and recoiling back upstream a bit *(Figure 7.4)*. This obvious slowing of the currents produces the hydraulic cushion at the face of the boulder. And fish love to lie on cushions and have their food brought to them. Always fish the hydraulic cushions.

When I'm tossing big leeches, like I was on the Madison a few paragraphs prior, this is one of the first places that I pitch a fly. And I like to do it in an almost straight-down approach, if possible. I cast the fly into the currents a few feet to the side of the boulder and just above it, and then allow the imitation to swing right into the cushion. I let it hang there, and then strip it upstream a bit. If there's a fish there, it will usually grab the big leech. Of course, one can drift or swing a dry or nymph into the cushion, as well.

When Jason and I were filming on the Varzina in Russia, we encountered a very wet and rainy day; cold, too. We decided to shoot along a series of rapids, where the somber day only added to the energy of the river. The water was deep—really deep—in the center, so I decided to fish the secret river and any boulders it contained. I fished down with a size 2 black leech and a big 3/0 shot clamped to the leader. We hit a couple of promising looking spots, but nothing. There was a nice boulder downstream, and I figured that a good fish would be holding in the cushion.

I made the cast, the fly swung into the cushion, the rod tip thumped down, and the fish jumped up. It was a big one, and when he crashed back into the water, we could hear his landing clearly through my mic—a deep, heavy smack. That's what I like!

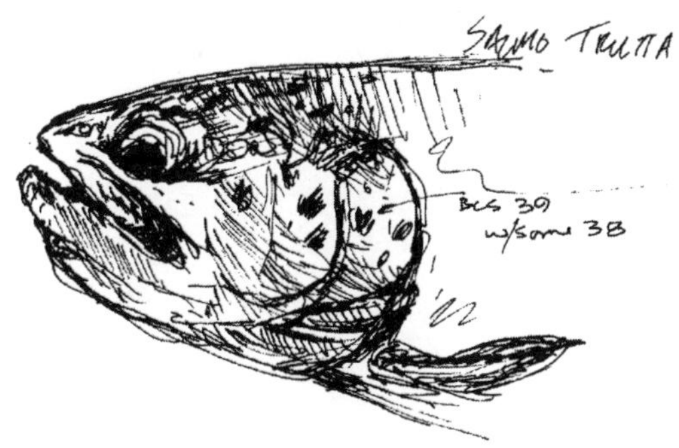

Other Stuff

It's not unusual to encounter rapids that curve or even make sharp bends. And it's not unusual to find all sorts of debris in rapids where it has caught up on the boulders or been jammed against a bank during high water. One may find undercut banks, gravel bars, islands, fallen trees, and all sorts of structure. Don't try to memorize a whole long list of items and how to fish around them. Rather, think about places out of the current with a supply of food coming in, or shallow areas with food—then go after them.

On the very top end of Russia's Sidorovka, the water runs in one series of rapids after another. The "pools" are more spots where the rapids hesitate for a second before tearing onward. Harsh winters can keep the big fish population knocked down, but there are still those 8- to 14-inchers in abundance. At its top end, the flow is 20 to 30 feet wide, so one can fish down and really hit every possible prime lie or feeding lie. It's rapid-fire fishing, almost like float fishing. Similar rivers can be fished the same way.

Cascades

A cascade is a rapids trying to be a waterfall. The bottom is very steeply inclined, and the water splashes down the channel with all the vigor of a waterfall, but without the vertical plunge. Cascades can form over bedrock—like those on the Gibbon River in Yellowstone Park—or they can simply be formed in a densely bouldered stretch of stream *(Figure 7.5)*.

Figure 7.5. *Cascades are rapids wanting to be waterfalls. If there's any deep water, there can be good fishing in the smoother areas between the drops.*

When the water tears down over bedrock, there are few a pockets that hold fish, and they can hold good ones. It can be dangerous fishing, however, because the smooth rock is a tough bottom to walk on, and the water is often pushier than most anglers are used to. Watch the edges of such areas, because there can be deeper pockets and undercuts if the stream is running through forestland.

When the water is a cascade among boulders, there are many pockets that one can explore with a nymph, long fly, or dry. The fishing is not a leisurely day astream, it's tough wading, quick casting, often difficult floats, but always interesting. Be careful in such waters, however. Because of the cascading nature of the stream, water can vary in depth from a few inches to many feet in a very short distance. One wrong step and one can be swimming right along with the fish!

Studying Runs & Flats, Sloughs & Backwaters

This is not really the "miscellaneous" category, it's just that all of these stream features have one thing in common: they generally exhibit relatively little surface variation. They can vary widely in depth, current speed, and bottom structure, but looking at the surface won't tell you much about these characteristics. Reading these waters requires a bit more probing to understand the underlying character of each of them.

Runs

Typically, runs are riffles that are too deep and perhaps a bit too slow to show standing waves at the surface, or they may be places where deep water moves quickly over bedrock, clay, or even gravels. A run might even be a rapids if it had big boulders in it. Unlike pools, which clearly show a deep belly, runs tend to be more or less uniform in depth from one end to the other—reluctant pools, perhaps. Runs also tend to be narrower than pools—think of them as chutes of water moving along at a nice uniform pace. And typically, the bottom is more "U" shaped than in other stream areas. In *The Trout and the Stream*, Charlie Brooks says of runs:

> "Runs are my favorite type of water, and I like them deep, three to five feet, fast enough to border on being rapids, with a rubble boulder bottom. Some Eastern friends look at the runs I take them to, and do label them rapids.

> Such runs in this country [around West Yellowstone, Montana—GB] hold the largest of the stone fly nymphs and also sculpins. They also hold fish up to five pounds. With the exception of weed beds, they are the most difficult of water types to fish. No one I know is really expert in fishing them and most anglers pass them by."

Runs can hold big fish because they are deep (providing good cover) and have a steady current that brings a constant flow of food. If the bottom has enough rocks, logs, or other obstructions to provide sufficient hydraulic protection, then it may hold a rather good number of bigger fish. When confronted with a run, I generally tend to fish the secret river along the edge on my side. Big fish can, and do, lie in the deep water out in the center of the current, but there's a far better chance of finding feeding fish in the zone of slower water along the shore lines.

A boulder-strewn run on Wisconsin's Wolf River.

Now, having said that, I will also admit to fishing the center water, too. I like to use a nymphing rig with shot and perhaps even weighted flies for such places. It's tough fishing because you've got to get the fly right on the bottom in the heavy flow (okay, within a foot of the bottom). This is a great place for a big black leech (a favorite "all conditions" fly). When I'm exploring for fish during opportunistic periods, I may choose to go with a nymph and indicator and take whatever comes along. This choice usually results in the most fish. But if I want the big boys, then I'll go with a big boy fly—maybe even two as I related in the last chapter.

Fish Boil

One of the unique features of runs, one that certainly falls within the skill of reading the surface to determine bottom structure, is the surface "boil" *(Figure 8.1)*. A boil occurs when water runs over the top of a bottom obstruction such as a boulder. There may be a small standing wave at the upstream edge of the boil, but then again, there may not be. As strong boil is formed when the obstruction is close to the surface. It will exhibit a great deal of surface disturbance. A soft boil occurs when the obstruction is deep, and the surface disturbance is only very slight. A boil always says, "fish here." There are two meanings of this call to the angler, (1) there are fish living here, (2) ply your flies through this water.

Figure 8.1. *A boil (arrows), with or without a standing wave, in a run or rapids is the sign of a bottom obstruction that creates an "underwater pool."*

Think of a boil as an underwater "pocket." It's just like a pocket behind a big rock in a rapids, but it's totally under the surface. That being the case, fish the current tongues on either side of the boil, and get the fly in the hydraulic slip behind the bottom obstruction, as well as in the hydraulic cushion ahead of it. A word of understanding here, however. Since one cannot necessarily see the obstruction, be ready to lose a few flies. If the unseen bottom obstruction is a big stump or log, well, goodbye to a fly or two. Even when the bottom object is a rock, the fly can hang up. Don't lament a lost fly or two because one can often haul out big fish from such places. What is a lost fly compared to the conquest of a trout in the two-foot class?

When Jason and I were fishing a big Russian river some years ago, the guides took us to the outfall of a lake on the flowage. It was very much a run. The water was quite deep and moved along briskly. There were big to huge boulders in the water and along the edges, but the bottom was not tipped enough to create rapids. The surface was smooth, with only a few ripples around the emergent boulders, but there were boils dotting the surface to indicate the positions of the big sunken rocks. It was full of big browns. It was wide, too—a full fly line in places—but the fish were cooperative, and they took leeches, scuplins and mice imitations very well. We fished our flies among the boulders along the far side, around the boils in mid-current, and even downstream over sunken boulders on our side. Our biggest fish was a "double-digit" (10+ pound) brown that fought very strongly in the heavy water.

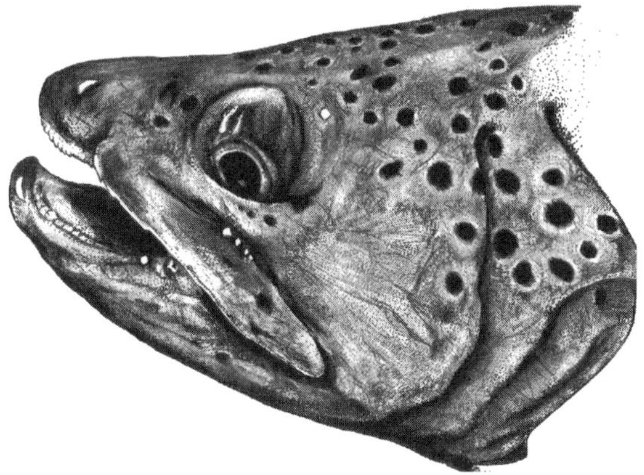

Spring Runs

To this point, I haven't singled out spring creeks because riffles, rapids, and pools operate the same, regardless of a stream's origins. But I have found that spring creeks have more runs than freestone streams. Spring creeks are usually valley features and cut through finer materials, tending to dig more uniformly deep channels. And, spring creeks seem, overall, to have more depth for their width than freestone streams. They certainly have more in-stream vegetation and generally more areas of silt and other fine materials than freestone streams.

Runs like this one on England's justly famous Itchen present a real challenge to anglers accustomed to the more lively character of freestoners.

Often, when confronted with this flow of deep water and vegetation, anglers that frequent freestoners find the whole thing a bit confusing, and go in search of areas that offer more familiar features, like pools and riffles. But, it pays to spend time studying the deeper runs because they can be places of big trout. If the weed beds are submerged, the surface will often display "boils." Since the water goes through the weeds as well as being deflected upward, these boils will be more subtle than those formed in the fast water runs of freestoners.

It is the subtle nature of such "soft" boils that often causes anglers their greatest frustration when fishing spring creeks. However, these soft boils can provide some of the most memorable experiences on such streams, too.

Browns on the Run

There's an incident that I described in my 1979 book, *Nymphing*, that clearly illustrates the potential of runs in spring creeks. In June of 1972, Nancy and Jason and I headed back to Pennsylvania from our new home in Wausau, Wisconsin, to visit our families. It was on this trip that I purchased an R.H. Woods cane rod. In addition to fishing Little Sandy and the other streams of my youth, I went to fish the fabled spring creeks of south-central Pennsylvania.

A deep, slow, weedy run with watercress overhanging the banks—perfect big-fish water.

I drove Nancy and Jason to New Jersey to be with Nancy's sister and family, and then headed out to camp and fish for a few days. I stopped at the Yellow Breeches Fly Shop and introduced myself to Ed Koch, who owned and operated the shop at that time. His book, *Fishing the Midge* had just been published, and I welcomed the opportunity to talk to him about the ins and outs of spring creek fishing.

We talked of flies and fishing in general, and I showed him some of my newer fly designs. It was a good couple of hours of just getting to know each other. I asked Ed if he knew a place I could camp, and he offered to let me park my van in the shop's parking lot. I had converted the inside of the van for camping (it was all do-it-yourself in those days), so I quickly took him up on his offer. He gave me some tips on places to go, and I went to sleep, content that I was going to have a great time fishing.

Well, the next morning I awoke to a huge lightning storm and absolutely pounding rain. I was glad I was in the van—at least I didn't have to go outside to get in the driver's seat. I decided to drive around and at least see the streams; certainly the storm would have blown them out. The Yellow Breeches was yellow with mud. Not a surprise. But it looked like great water. I headed on over to Big Spring. I'd been there once before on a field trip from the Mont Alto campus of Penn State ten years earlier, and had seen big trout feeding in several flats. As I drove up the river, I stopped and looked at the water, but the pounding rain kept me in the truck with the windows rolled up tight.

Very near the top end, I pulled into a small parking area to look at the stream. It danced over a bit of a riffle, and then turned sharply toward the parking lot in a deep run. The far side was overgrown with watercress, and the currents at the top of the run slid under the bright green vegetation. As I reached for the key to restart the van and move on, the rain stopped. A few sprinkles dripped down, and then it was over. The sky was still cloudy, but it was warm and without any wind. I hopped out for a closer look. The water was clear, rising perhaps, but the vegetated valley had prevented soil runoff.

As I stood there looking, it dawned upon me that I might have the perfect opportunity. It was overcast, the water was rising slightly, and there was a great piece of water right there in front of me. I grabbed the rod and my vest, and set up my nymphing rig with a Red Brown Nymph. I stood right in front of the van and cast up to the very top of the run where the currents ran under the cress. The fly drifted a couple of feet and the indicator jerked under. It was a very nice brown of about 2¼ pounds.

I decided to see if lightning would strike twice, and chucked the fly up to the top of the run once again. A repeat performance, but this time the fish was a 4-pound hen that fought deep and strong. It had a small head and deep, round body. Now the run really had my attention!

I decided to fish it more. A few casts later and the indicator dipped under again. This time, the fish jumped and ran up to the top of the run, then back, twisting and flexing powerfully in the current. The little cane rod strained as I put pressure on the fish to keep it away from the cress. It continued to fight deep along the bottom of the run, twisting this way and that, but eventually came to the net—another 4-pound hen. Like the previous fish it had a small head and huge body. It was a young fish that had more than plenty to eat. I was thrilled, to say the least.

I fished the run for another half-hour without a take, and decided to move down. I was not wearing waders, there was no need to. Then I spotted another run that seemed to say, "This is the spot, cast here." I did. Again the indicator shot under. On the hook set, the fish took off like a torpedo. Pound for pound, it fought far harder than the other three, but eventually the 2¾-pound brown succumbed to the strain of the cane.

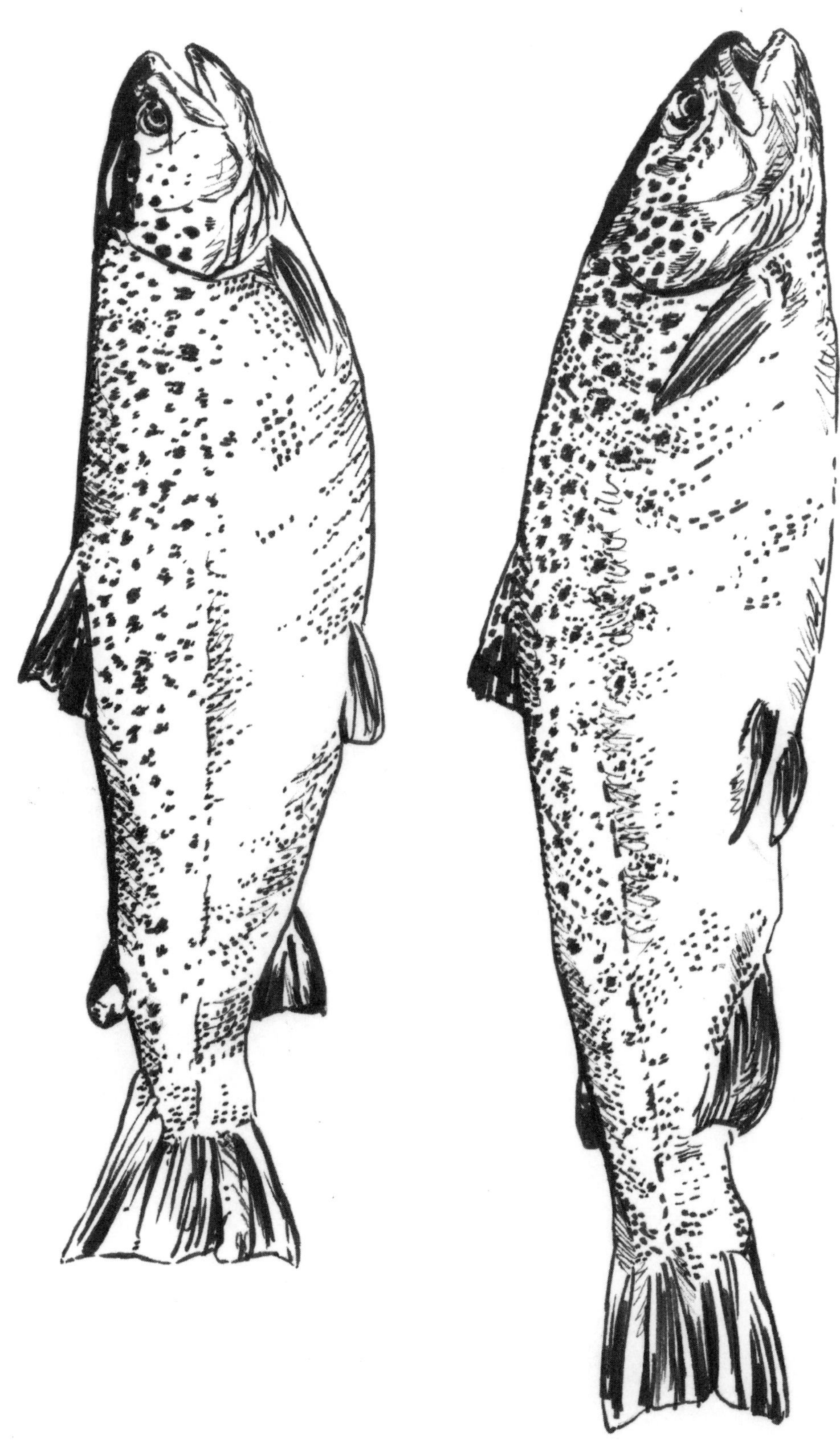

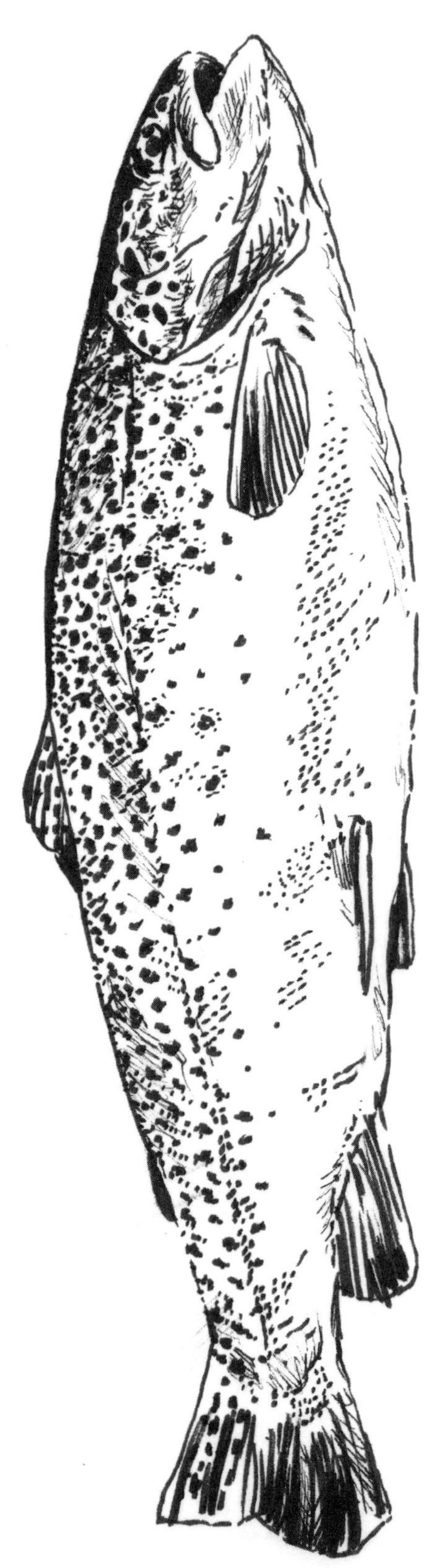

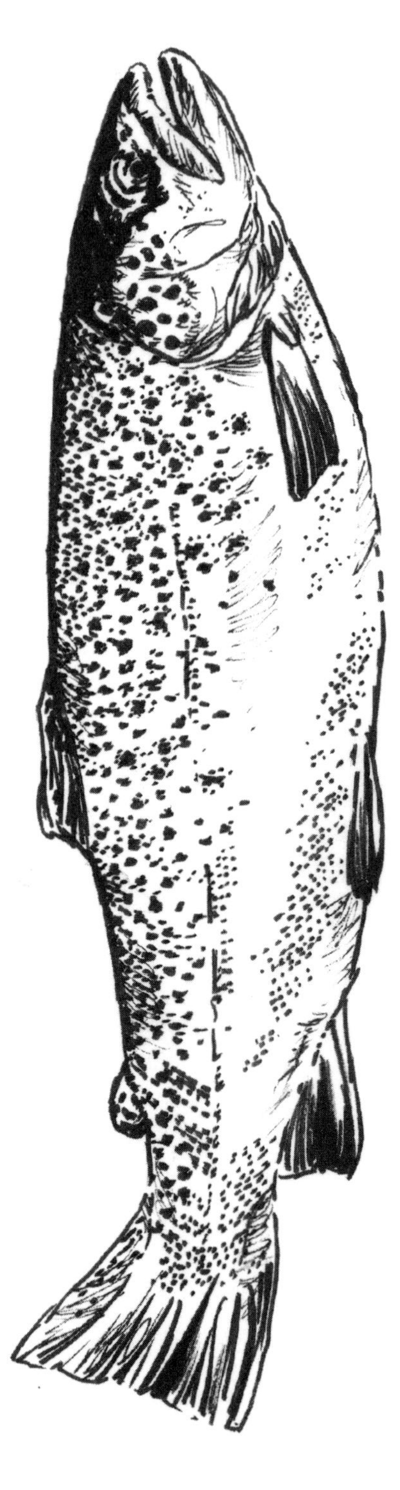

Then, suddenly, the clouds broke and bright sun lit the water. The fishing was over, but I stuck with it for another half hour, just to be certain. Four big fish between 10:30 and noon, and I'd never even put on my waders. That's the potential of runs.

Flats

I learned about flats early on. My parents lived within walking distance of Sugar Creek in Venango County, Pennsylvania, between two bridges; one about a half mile upstream and the other a mile downstream. That's the water I fished most. Sugar Creek had all the stream features, and I fished them all. Flats were my least favorite because in those days I didn't really appreciate (or understand) the subtleties of fishing them. But I was to learn.

Flats are exactly like they sound—flat. They are places generally where the stream is relatively shallow and spread out *(Figure 8.2)*. The flow is greatly slowed because of the increased width. And, because of the width, everything in the flat is fully exposed to overhead predators. One finds only spooky fish out in the open waters of the flat. A fly line whizzing overhead will put such fish on a run for cover before the angler ever knows they're there. There can be brush, trees, overhanging grasses, debris piles, boulders, logs, and other items along the shore line, and occasionally in mid stream, where fish can find prime lies. So, like runs, flats deserve more attention than most anglers give them.

Figure 8.2. *Flats are exactly what their name suggests. Fish can be incredibly spooky in these places.*

Comeuppance

One hot, sticky summer day in my teen years I wandered up to one of the bridges on Sugar Creek. The currents at the bridge were lovely. There was a nice riffle that started a 100 yards above, some deep cuts, and a big pool below. But further up was a long, long flat. There was some "good" water above that, and I decided to head on up and fish the riffles that came down into the head of the flat.

I was wading slowly because rubber-soled hippers do not allow one to wade fast. River right was overhung with alders, grasses, stinging nettles, and other vegetation. River left was a cow pasture that was much more grassy, and without the heavy brush. I plodded along in the sticky heat, not looking for fish, but just trying to get up stream to the riffles. Normally, I'd jump out and walk the pasture up, but this day I was wading along slowly, keeping my legs cool. Over along the far side, just in the shadow of the brush, I noticed a bunch of chubs feeding. I was deadly on chubs. Thank goodness they were abundant in Sugar Creek; they at least gave me some entertainment between the occasional hits from trout. I decided to catch a couple of them.

I unloaded a cast in their direction. The little dry floated along and then disappeared. I used my best chub set, which in those days was designed to aerialize them. The tippet parted with a shot, and a huge brown tore out from under the brush and rocketed off upstream to places unknown. I was stunned and cursed myself under my breath. I stopped aerializing chubs.

Boiling Flats

In small to medium freestone streams, flats seem to be more night feeding spots than daytime hangouts. One can find exceptions, certainly, especially if the flats are more than knee deep. But it seems from all the fishing I've done around the world, that flats are most important in spring creeks and big rivers. Fishing the really big waters is the subject of the next chapter, so we'll address their flats there, but I do want to spend some time looking at flats in spring creeks in this chapter.

Spring creeks are typically plant infested when compared with freestone streams, and the weed beds completely change the character of flats. Every weed bed is a sheltering lie, and if the water is deep enough, can even provide prime lies for the fish.

Henry's Fork is a unique spring creek; it's actually a tailwater fishery and a spring creek fishery at the same time. Tailwaters are basically the same as spring creeks if the water is drawn off the bottom of the pool above the dam—really a reservoir—and the dam on Henry's Fork is exactly that, a bottom draw dam. The water comes out cold and nutrient laden. Then just a good long spit downstream, the Buffalo enters. It's 100-percent spring creek, and one can drive to the originating springs and watch big trout finning in the crystalline currents.

Watching big fish do their thing is always time well-spent.

By the way, watching big fish is always time well spent. Not just so you get to see big fish, but so you can watch how and where they hold. Most anglers do not spend nearly enough time really observing fish. They just go fishing with a vague sort of hope that somehow, today will be the day. Take it from someone who spent a childhood lifetime hoping that the next day would be the day. It doesn't work. Better to spend the time learning about the fish and its food, and then applying that knowledge through a predatory filter.

Mike Lawson's book, *Spring Creeks*, is a veritable cornucopia of information on spring creeks, using Henry's Fork as the focal point. Although there is not a chapter, *per se*, devoted strictly to reading spring creeks, there is much information in his chapter on "Presentation" that is devoted to the nuances of reading waters of this stream type.

In the Railroad Ranch section of the Fork (now, Harriman State Park) the river runs through the ash of ancient volcanoes. There's a bit of gravel, some basaltic rock, a couple of deep holes, and what might even be classified as a minor rapids just above the Osborne Bridge, but basically this section of the river is one giant flat. A flat of nearly uniform depth—one can wade it nearly anywhere—and a flat filled with undulating aquatic plants.

The surface looks extremely smooth, but it is infinitely deceptive. Anglers not familiar with the Fork immediately assume that smooth means no drag. You remember the old caution about assuming? If you want to make any assumptions that have a factual basis, then *always* assume you're going to have drag, and then do everything in your skill base to eliminate or minimize it.

The weeds in the river are waving for a reason: the currents are making them wave. If the weeds are waving, then the currents are also causing an almost infinite variety of minor cross currents, eddies, zig-zags, reverses, and every other type of bizarre current distortion that one can think of—even some you can't think of. These are all a form of a "boil," as the water pushes through the weeds, and in so doing, is forced to the surface. Many of the surface currents that are created this way are small, but have a real effect, none the less. Such micro-currents make the Fork the ultimate test for the person who wants to learn drag-free fishing in the film. This is the river made for the Down-and-Across Dead Drift approach. The fly is presented down-and-across stream on a Parachute Mend. Cast, pull the rod back and up as the line is extending. When the line drops to the water, the rod tip is then lowered to feed the slack into the drift just a bit faster than the currents are taking it away.

Typically, I cast five to six feet above the fish and past its feeding lane, adding the Parachute Mend into the mix. Even after the mend, the fly lands a foot or so beyond the feeding lane. The rod is held still until the fly skates back out, right into the feeding lane, and then the rod tip is lowered. The fly drifts down to the fish, without drag. The fish sees the fly before it sees the line and leader. There are a number of variations on this tactic and some others that work well, too, in our book, *Fishing the Film*.

The Harriman Ranch section of Henry's Fork is deceptively smooth looking. In fact, its surface is a turmoil of delicate, confused currents that create instant drag for the uninitiated fly fisher. Here, a rather young Jason is shown fishing with a down-and-across approach.

On Henry's Fork I prefer to fish the "stream-within-a-stream" (more on this concept coming up), focusing on the very catchable "bank feeders," rather than wandering around out in the currents trying for the occasional risers. Those are the "sucker fish" that draw one away from the real fishing along the banks. There are some exceptions. Good fish can feed in turbulence lines out in the main river, but even there, the fish that need to be marked and worked are the ready risers—the ones that have an established feeding rhythm. Otherwise, it's usually a waste of time.

Cruisin' the Flats

I cannot think of one of the many spring creeks that I have fished across the globe that doesn't have flats worthy of attention. One of the typical events that I've seen on spring creek flats is the cruising rise. Trout will often cruise up current, rising as they go, and then drift back with the currents, not feeding, and then cruise up, feeding again. The very first time I saw this, I though that I had a series of trout rising in a feeding lane. But then, no rises, and after a bit, the fish at the bottom rose, followed in perfect progression by the fish above it. "Wait a minute," I said to myself, "there's no 'synchronous feeding' in the fish Olympics." "It's one fish looking like many."

If the water in a flat is slow enough, then one can encounter random risers that are simply swimming around as if they were in a stillwater situation. One really needs to see the fish in order to know where to cast next. Fortunately, in such slow water, if the wind is not a problem, seeing the fish is not terribly difficult, even on an overcast day. The cast needs to land far enough ahead of the fish so that line impact is not an issue, and yet in a position that seems to be on an intercept line with the cruising fish.

There's a story in *Fishing the Film* about Jason and me fishing in Tasmania for big browns in very shallow water and suspending the nymph only four to six inches under an indicator. That was in a flat shortly after the river emerged from a large lake.

Flat Pockets

Sometimes flats will have pockets or slots in them, too. These are fish magnets, and should never go unfished. One late season I was fishing the Norfork in Arkansas. The generators were not running, and so many of the runs and pools became flats. Where do the trout go when the water drops a foot or two? Well, they go into any deeper water they can find. This cold November day I found them along a series of bedrock slots where the water was two to three feet deep.

There was a good midge hatch (as there often is on tailwaters around the world), and I was looking for snouts. I nearly stumbled into the first slot. Only a couple of feet wide, and nearly as deep, it got my immediate attention. As I watched it, sure enough, a nose poked out upstream about 20 feet. From then on, I concentrated on the slots and did very well, indeed.

It's easier to stay warm when the flats fishing is hot.

Other times, I've fished the White River very near the Norfork and found similar situations. One day, in warmer weather, I was poking around looking for fish in the White's giant flats, when I saw a rise very near shore. There was actually dry, exposed bedrock between the main current and this tiny back current along the bank. None-the-less, the back channel was a series of little pockets in the rock, and they were full of fish feeding ever so delicately on midges. And boy, were they spooky. Suddenly, I was forced to fish on my knees, casting sidearm with a long tippet and a tiny midge imitation. It was a tough, but fulfilling day.

Sloughs & Backwaters

For angling purposes, these are the same, but for wading, they are not. Sloughs are areas that open into the stream, and which are swampy, marshy, or boggy. A swamp is a wetland with trees, a marsh is a wetland with cattails, a bog is a wetland with sphagnum moss. They're all wet and juicy and have the potential to swallow up a careless wader. We have plenty of these sloughs here in Wisconsin, and one must always be extra careful when wading in them. Careful not to get stuck, but careful not to telegraph one's presence to the fish, either. It's very easy to do in such mushy soil. There are some great spring ponds that are best fished out of a float-tube or canoe simply because walking the edges spooks everything within casting distance. A backwater is like a slough with no mushy soil. Oh, maybe a spot here and there, but not the sticky, nasty smelling goo that one finds along a slough.

Sloughs and backwaters may not always look like much, but they can sometimes offer fantastic angling opportunities. Here, Dave Gourley nets a big rainbow taken from what some might dismiss as "frog water."

On one of the streams in Wisconsin that I fish regularly, there's a deep hole about a mile above the nearest bridge. One must canoe into the spot. On river right, there's most definitely a slough. One does not go wading in there. It's big, and there's a bit of an "island" in the center—more of a slight high spot with grasses growing on it. One cannot stand on it without sinking in to one's armpits. But the water around the island holds the biggest fish in the pool—at night. During the day, they're out there on the bottom of the pool or up under the deep chute of rapids that dumps in at the top.

That slough has yielded more big fish than any other place on the river. I wish I could say that I discovered the slough's big-fish secret, but I did not. My colleague and fishing friend, Ed Osypowski, was the one who figured it out.

Ed had wanted to learn to tie a few flies, so I showed him a way to dress a *Hexagenia* dry. It was June and the big bugs were out in full force. Well, his first fly didn't even come close. In fact, after seeing it we named it the "Polish Warbonnet." Ed took his wild and crazy fly up to the big pool and fished the slough with it. We figured that there were a lot of big fish in that pool, and I think Ed caught every one of them that summer—all at night, all in the slough, and all on the "Bonnet."

Feeding Line

In my book, *Presentation*, I told a story about fishing for king salmon with my friend, Jim Hagar, in Alaska. It's a good story to segue into the next chapter on big rivers, and it's also instructive of what one can find at the edge, where a backwater or slough intersects the main current (It's a turbulence line, a seam, a fish magnet).

It was the third night of our Alaskan float trip with Wayne Dawson's Headwaters Expeditions, and as we beached the rafts on a gravel bar along the Salmon River, Jim excitedly pointed downstream and yelled out, "Did you see that salmon?" "It was a huge king, and it jumped completely out of the water!"

"There's a big slough down there," noted our guide, Dennis. "The salmon school up there, but in this high water, it's going to be hard to find a place to cast from."

Hard was right! I knew that fish would be resting in the seam where the deep, fast currents of the river swept past the slowly reversing waters of the immense slough. I also knew from the previous three days' fishing that the big kings would take a black Strip Leech if I could get it on the inside edge of the seam and retrieve it past them slowly. But to be effective, I'd have to cast the whole fly line, and casting room was at a premium. High brush and trees, some fallen into the river, prevented a long back cast, and the large fly and two, size 3/0 split shot (needed to keep the fly down at the fish's level) made long-distance roll casting tough, even with the 10-foot, 7 weight.

The solution was not to try to cast a whole line. The solution was to use the river to do my work for me. I stood on the point and made a thirty-foot cast down and across the swift water of the main river. At the end of the stroke, I added a Reach Mend to position the line in the fast flow and immediately began stripping line off the reel and feeding it into the current with a flopping mend. Within seconds, the whole line had been fed downstream. Then, by walking a couple of steps toward the slow waters of the slough, I was able to use the drag of the currents to swing the line into the seam.

Hooking the line under a finger of my rod hand, I began a slow strip, retrieving about a foot of line in three seconds and then stopping for three seconds. On the third strip, the line jerked tight, and I pulled the hook home with a strip strike. The 30-pound king burst from the water in an awkward half jump as Jim laughed in mock exasperation, "I don't believe it, I don't believe it."

Even though I fought the fish with side pressure from the butt of the big rod, stressing the tippet to the edge of its breaking strength, it was still 10 minutes before I could work the big male close enough for Jim to tail it. As he knelt by the sharply sloping mud bank of the slough, I reeled the fish to within two feet of the rod tip and then slowly backed away, guiding the big salmon toward Jim with side pressure from the rod butt. Raising the rod tip to pull the fish close would have been a mistake; such a move would have taken pressure off the fish, giving it control and allowing it to swim beyond reach. And since the tip is not strong enough to pull such a large fish close, attempting to do so could have broken the rod. (Two other anglers on the trip broke rods trying to use the tip to land big kings.)

It took a few minutes and some careful rod usage, but the big king was eventually to hand. Here, reading waters was more important in getting the fly to the right spot than it was for finding fish.

After the release, it was Jim's turn, and he repeated my success on his very first cast/reach/feed/swing/slow retrieve. Our excited hollers and congratulations got the attention of the others, and they quickly discovered that the slough was filled with cruising salmon. It was a night all of us will remember. And though it was hard to leave, there were other backwaters ahead, and everyone now knew the technique for reaching those distant salmon in the seam.

I use this Feeding Line Tactic for many other situations, too. It's a great way to work the fly back under overhanging vegetation or to get the fly into otherwise impossible spots. It works with dry flies, nymphs, minnow imitations, leeches, mice, or any other fly; and it works whether fishing on the bottom or at the film. It's effective whether the fly is being fished with action or dead drifted. It works to swing the fly (as with the salmon) or to feed the imitation down a single current lane. It's just a good all around tactic that the fly fisher can use to great benefit in many situations.

Big Waters

Most people who think of trout fishing envision streams in the 30- to 100-foot wide category, with wadable riffles and a few deep pools and runs. And there are plenty of trout streams just like that. But then, there are the big waters, clearly rivers, not even close to the "stream" category in sheer size and water volume. Most fly fishers would rather head to streams, spring creeks, brooks, and other smaller waters than wade into big streams, rivers, and what can only be termed "super-rivers." But these big waters can hold truly big fish and plenty of them. The problem, for most anglers, is the sheer size of the river. Smaller streams are relatively easy to read, but the big flows are threateningly encyclopedic in size, appearing to offer no firm starting point for reading waters.

French Creek & the Allegheny

I was most fortunate to have spent my youth near the confluence of French Creek and the Allegheny River. Sugar Creek (my home water, as I've noted before) had its confluence with French Creek at the town of Sugar Creek, where I went to grade school. French Creek poured into the Allegheny at Franklin, where I went to high school. I knew them all well and fished them every chance I got.

French Creek really qualifies as a river. It's well over a hundred feet wide and its water volume averages around 3,300 cubic feet per second (cfs). Sugar Creek, which is definitely a solid "stream," runs at about one-fourth of that volume. But then comes the Allegheny at nearly 16,000 cfs on average. What does one do when confronted with such enormous volumes of water? The secret to reading all big rivers is to read the stream-within-a-stream.

Rather than trying to read the vastness of all the water all at once, read it a bit at a time. And only read that bit which you can easily and safely fish. Just because the river is a half-mile or more wide doesn't mean you're going to fish the full width. Don't worry about the potential of the water that can't be reached. Rather, concentrate on that part of the river that you have access to, reading it just like any other water of casting-distance width.

On big rivers like the Yellowstone, read the water that can be fished and don't worry about the rest.

When I was old enough to drive, I used to love to go to French Creek just upstream from Utica, and fish for smallmouth bass. There were many places where one could fish, but we'd found a riffle that dumped into a big pool that was particularly kind to us. It was an evening fishery, and in the summer, after a hot day of haying for a neighboring farmer or working for my father's roofing company, we'd hit French Creek, wet wading and casting for smallies. They would move up out of the deep hole and feed in the riffles, and we'd go after them with a spinning rod and a MirrOLure, or a fly rod and big white Marabou Muddler, a Mickey Finn, or other long fly. That section of the riffle was about 50 feet wide and 100 feet long, and we'd spend a couple of hours there working those bass. That spot never failed to give us great action.

The Allegheny was another story. It was composed of monster pools, mile-long runs, threatening rapids, and flats that defy description. But when one fished it, it was the edges that showed the character that we could fish. There were plenty of gravel bars, cuts, pockets and other such stream features in the stream-within-a-stream, and that's where we fished.

Trout fishermen that were "in the know" would visit the rocky shoreline of the Allegheny and search under the stones and rocks right at waterline for big Hellgrammite larvae, which they would hook through the thorax and fish dead drift in trout streams for big browns. I remember a large, white, wash basin full of big browns that a neighbor had taken on Six-Mile Run. There, in the bottom of the wash basin, drifting among the big fish were a half dozen Hellgrammite larvae, which he specifically pointed out as his "secret" bait, describing where he collected them, how he rigged them, and where he fished them. It was certainly a mind-opening experience.

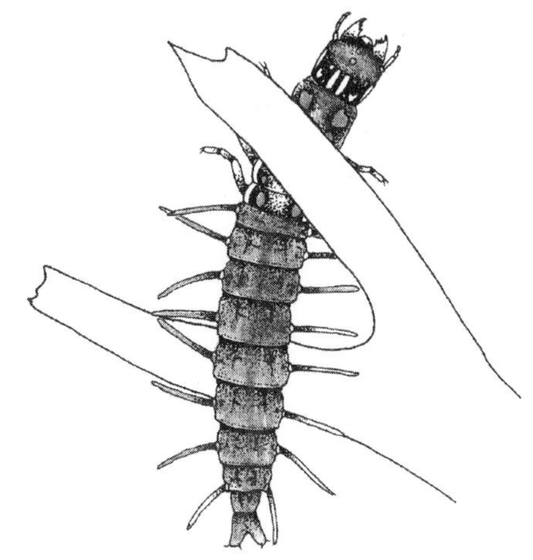

Among our favorite places on the Allegheny were the pools dug by the gravel dredging operations. A barge would sit near the shoreline and dredge gravel all day long. After the workday, the dredge would shut down, but the fishing would start. Smallmouth bass and walleyes loved the hole that was dug and the constant erosion at the upstream edge of the underwater pit, which was constantly shedding rocks and gravel under the pressure of the current. As a consequence of this erosive process, there was a constant stream of food pouring into the man-made hole. It was very good fishing there, when we could get to it.

In 1965, the Kinzua dam was completed on the Allegheny near Warren, Pennsylvania. It created Pennsylvania's deepest lake (the Allegheny Reservoir) and converted a stretch of the river from a warm-water fishery to a cold-water fishery. The river boasts browns in the 5- to 7-pound class. Like all the really big waters, many anglers float to fish. This is a good tactic because it allows the fly rodder to find the stream-within-a-stream that is most conducive to feeding lies and prime lies for big fish. Even more importantly, it allows the anglers to access bank cover and in-shore lies more easily than wading.

Night fishing can be excellent in this stretch of the river, not all that far from Jim Bashline's favorite Goodsell pool. A boat in these big waters also allows the fly fisher to access mid-stream gravel bars and other features that simply are beyond the reach of the wading angler. But even in mid-river situations, the angler still reads the water as a stream-within-a-stream, searching for the most ideal piece of water containing all the food concentrating features that draw feeding trout.

Newhalen and Kvichak

The last several miles of the Newhalen form a broad estuary-type river that is up to 400 or more yards wide. This, the largest tributary to Lake Iliamna, drains Lake Clark through Six Mile Lake, and for the last 24 miles before entering the estuarial zone consists of monster rapids. It gets an enormous run of sockeye each year, headed to the tributaries of Six Mile and Clark lakes. And, of course, it gets a great run of big Iliamna rainbows following the salmon. This is the site of the story, "Spooled," in Chapter One.

There's great fishing in these waters between the canyon mouth and the big lake. Because the river both widens and slows dramatically, there are many mid-stream gravel bars where one can find huge schools of sockeye hanging out. There, the big trout also park, eating eggs and porking-up for the coming winter. Many of the gravel bars slope off sharply into deep water on the downstream edge, providing a spot very much like the upstream lip of a pool. This is always a good place to find trout waiting for drifting eggs. Of course the deep-water runs between the bars are also good.

My wife, Nancy, into a big rainbow in the estuary region of the Newhalen. She focused only on the water that was easily reached and read.

As big as the Newhalen is, it is not anywhere near the size of the Kvichak that drains lake Iliamna. The Kvichak gives up many rainbows over 10 pounds each year. It should. The big fish from Iliamna back down into the river to feed. There are huge holes and runs where the river dumps out of the lake, and Trevor Goudy and I filmed part of a TV show there, working hard for the big rainbows in an early June cold spell. But our best fish came from down river.

Like many Alaskan rivers, the Kvichak has a braided section where it divides into a series of smaller streams separated by islands of all sizes. Here the waters are more "stream" sized, and offer the fly fisher classic water consisting of riffles, pools, runs, and flats. There are good hatches here, too, and one can find rainbows feeding at the film in early season. On any big river, if one can find islands, then one has basically found the stream-within-a-stream and can more easily locate the places where fish might be holding. Besides, trout like such back channels because they offer softer currents and an easier place to find food.

When the smolt run comes to the Alaskan streams in June—young salmon drifting out to sea—look out. There will be big trout tearing the little fish out of the surface with great regularity. It can easily fool the fly fisher (I raise my hand as one fooled) into thinking the fish are eating insects that are hatching.

When we were shooting the TV show, we wanted to illustrate a way to figure out what the fish were taking. We'd found a channel that held some big fish feeding with vigor at the film, and I used a small screen that fit over my net to sample the currents. There were some caddis pupae husks, but also drifting smolts. We took the smolts to shore, and I tied a fly on the spot to mimic them, then used the fly to catch a couple of nice trout. The biggest one we saw feeding, however, eluded us.

The next evening, at dinner, the young son of another guest at the Alaska Sportsman's Lodge, where we were staying, reported that he'd caught the big fish on a size 10, Gold Ribbed Hare's Ear Nymph, fished with a down-and-across swing just under the surface. It was a 27-inch rainbow, full bodied and strong. In late season, after a full summer of eating salmon eggs, it might have weighed in between 9 and 10 pounds, but in early June it weighed about 7 pounds—still a very nice fish. Since the Hare's Ear could have suggested either a caddis pupa or a smolt, one can never be 100 percent certain what the rainbow thought it was eating, but my bet would be on the smolt. I've seen such feeding other times, and once the smolt run starts, the fish really focus on them, to the absolute neglect of all other food.

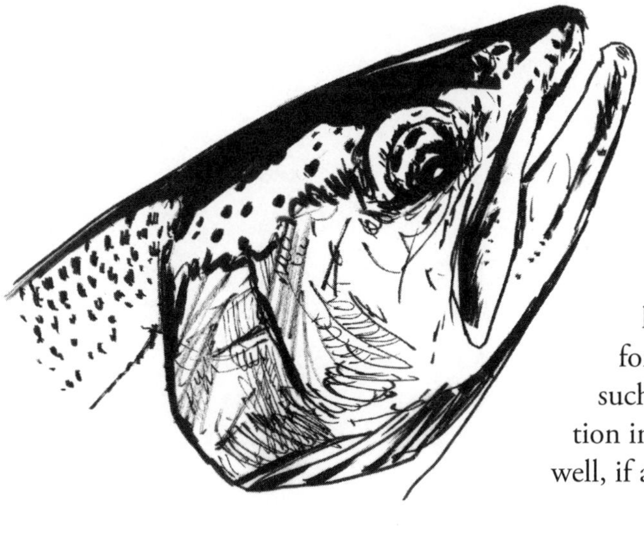

The main stem of the Kvichak holds plenty of rainbows, too. Again, the idea is not to worry about what you can't fish, but rather to worry about the water that you can fish. Dave Graebel and I were staying at No-See-Um Lodge on the Kvichak during the king salmon and sockeye salmon runs. In the near-shore zone on each side of the huge river, sockeye streamed in by the hundreds of thousands, headed up river to the headwater streams of Iliamna, Six Mile, Clark, Gibraltar, and other lakes of the drainage. We'd fish for them in the evenings, but when such fish are running with a destination in mind, they don't take the fly well, if at all. So, in the evenings, rather than get frustrated with not catching the sockeyes, I'd put on a big articulated leech and fish for the rainbows.

There were any number of gravel bars to provide sharp drop-offs and breaks in the shoreline where coffin corners would form. I'd throw long and allow the fly to sweep the water all the way back to shore, take two steps down and repeat the process. I didn't take any 10-pounders, but I did take fish in the 4 to 6 pound range. They certainly fought hard enough in the big water.

Another year, near the end of the week, the chums started in. They were mixed with the sockeye, and when one of them grabbed the swinging fly, it was really exciting. They would rip off full bore, jump, greyhound, and generally make themselves really hard to get to shore. Perfect!

Chobe and Zambeze

The Chobe River in Botswana is a sizable river intersecting the even larger Zambezi, which is the fourth largest river in Africa. The Chobe flows through Chobe National Park, renown for its large herds of wild elephants. That's all well and good, and a river tour of the Park is fun for a day, but it was the tigers—tiger*fish*, that is—that we had come for. We stayed at Ralph and Dawn Oxenham's Ichingo Lodge on Impalila Island in Namibia, right on the shores of the Chobe. There were rapids just below camp, and then a big corner pool with waters to at least 20 feet deep. We fished it with 30-foot, lead-core heads and the biggest flies we had. I had a couple of strong pulls in the deep belly of the pool and a couple more back in the tailout region, but no fish.

The Chobe is big water that feeds the even bigger Zambezi.

The next day, one of the guides, Guy Lobjoit and I floated down the Chobe to the Zambezi and then fished up the Zambezi to a pick up point where we traveled back to camp by Land Rover. We pounded all the likely spots, and managed a couple of little fish in the 4- to 5-pound range. But there were bigger fish in those waters, and we knew it. When we came to the juncture of the rivers, there was our old friend, the confluence line. But what a confluence line. It was a couple of hundreds yards long and filled with foam. The currents ground and danced. If there were tigers in "them thar waters," this was the spot.

Guy pitched a big fly in the currents, and it was immediately grabbed by a nice tiger. It was about 15 pounds, and it jumped sky high and took off out into the big waters of the Zambezi, whipping the line across the boat. It immediately tangled on the boatman, catching him across the neck. He grabbed the line to prevent getting a line burn, and the leader broke. But the confluence line had come through. No matter how big the river systems, confluence lines are always good fishing lines.

Clutha

It's the second biggest river in New Zealand, discharging nearly 22,000 cfs at its mouth. And, it's a trout stream; actually, it's a trout river. It's great size makes it a bit threatening to the first time fly fisher, until one goes at it with the stream-within-a-stream attitude.

On one trip to the Clutha's waters, we maneuvered our Land Rover off the main highway and up the two-track, headed over the hill toward the valley of the river. It really was a two-track, and we were glad that we had 4-wheel capability. The sand, gullies, large rocks, and other obstructions in the "road" would have been impossible to navigate otherwise. We crept down the hill to the river, and parked in a level spot next to the water.

The brown inhaled the Manuka Beetle and fought me down a long stretch of very big water (note the size of the main river in the background).

We were parked on the inside corner of a huge bend with a high gravel bank on the outside corner. It was a good spot because the stream-within-a-stream on my side had shallows, pockets, and gravel bars that provided plenty of feeding lies. Only a short distance upstream, I spotted a nice brown just a few feet from the shore, finning quietly in a little coffin corner.

He came up and took a Manuka Beetle pattern on the first drift. Off into the big water at the hook set, he gave me a good run for my money—about 100 yards down before he hit the meshes of the net. Coffin corners are great spots even on the biggest of waters.

Bighorn

Jason was 16, and we had joined forces to produce a series of instructional videotapes. I had tried professional cameramen, but they weren't exactly what I needed. They certainly shot technically excellent footage, but they couldn't anticipate what I was going to do, or what the fish was going to do. I had told Jason that he could shoot some footage, and if it was any good, I would include a short piece in one on my productions. Well, as it turned out, Jason knew exactly what I was going to do, and he certainly knew what the fish were going to do. Suddenly I had my cameraman, and I had a director. He could put me and/or the camera in the right place and shoot exactly what was needed.

But today, it was his turn to fish and my turn to squint. We were fishing the Bighorn, and we wanted to show a variety of tactics with a variety of imitations. We'd come around a corner, and before us lay a broad riffle with a deep run on river right. It was grasshopper time, and I didn't want any boats drifting over the shallow water. We rowed into the deep run and shot into the pool below, cut across the river and beached the boats at the very bottom of the riffles. We got out, and taking advantage of the streamside brush to hide us, we worked our way up stream to a point where we could clearly see into the river.

We watched and watched. Suddenly there was a rise, and then another. Then as we continued to watch, we saw fish finning in the currents—it was going to be a great day.

The Bighorn is big water, but it provides some great fishing to those who are willing to read the stream-within-a-stream as Nancy has done here.

I set the camera as close to the water as possible without getting close enough to spook the fish. It was on the outside of the corner, so I could shoot right down the current as Jason fished up. We'd spotted a couple of nice fish, and Jason had their positions marked by bushes on the shore. At my yell of "Action," Jason began wading up and casting his hopper directly at the camera. On his third cast, the fly dropped above the position of the first fish he had marked, and a big head poked out and ate it. That's the way I like to shoot footage!

Bow

It was still grasshopper time, and Jason and I were floating another river—Canada's Bow, the Bighorn's "sister river." Like the 'horn, it has hundred-yard-long pools, flats, riffles, rapids, high banks, islands, and all the features that make for great fishing. But, when fishing hoppers, a very specific feature made all the difference in the world. There was a sharp drop-off four to five feet out from the shoreline. The water at the edge of the drop-off went from about one foot in depth to three or four feet deep. That's where the fish were. The fly had to drift exactly along that edge. If the fly was drifting along over the shallow water of the ledge, nothing. If the fly was more than a couple of feet out beyond the edge, nothing. It had to be right on the edge. And that's what we did.

Of course, if there was a gravel bar out in the river's center, or an island, we'd fish there, too. Many anglers think that hoppers are creatures of the shoreline, but they can get into mid-river very easily. They can fly, and getting to the center of the river is simply a matter of flying. Grasshoppers don't know that a river is a water-course filled with trout that want to eat them. To them it's just a spot down there to land. So, fish in mid-river also know about hoppers, and eat them, too. Fish that are down in deep pools, however, typically won't come up through the great depth of the water to eat hoppers. They move to spots where hoppers can be intercepted easily and where there's cover. That's why they were lying in the deep water on the outside edge of the in-shore lip, around gravel bars and islands. The whole length of such places offer potential prime lies, and they were filled with fish, eating hoppers. All we had to do to find them was to understand the simple needs of protection first, food second, both together best.

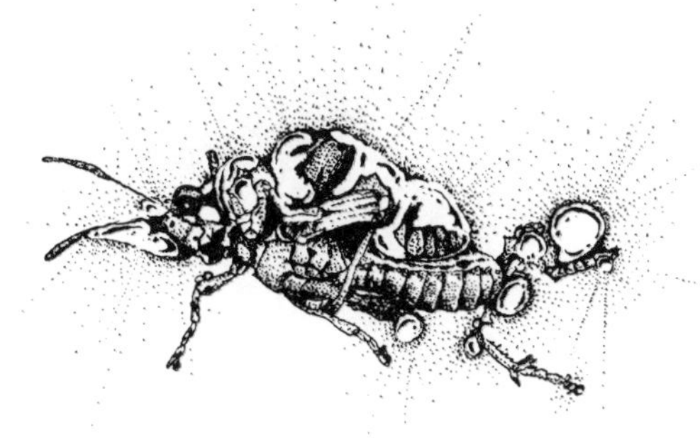

But there's much more to the Bow than hopper fishing. It's is a big river with big fish, and one can find them eating PMDs in side channels, sucking Tricos off the tailout of a huge pool, crunching caddis in the eddy swirls along a high bank, and nailing big baitfish and leeches everywhere. Read the stream-within-a-stream and allow it to show you where, when, what, and how to fish it.

White

Nancy and Jason and I had escaped the Wisconsin winter and were spending a week fishing in the early spring of Missouri. There were leaves coming out on the trees, and flowers, and green grass. They seemed novel to those of us from the frozen north; and besides that, it was warm. I had heard of the White for many years, but this was my first time to fish it. I wanted to get a first-hand feel for the water and the fishing, so I decided to wade and fish just below Table Rock Dam.

We broke camp early and headed to the river. It was big, but when we arrived the generators were off, and the water was running at a most wadable level. At first I just waded around a bit, looking at the water. When one is confronted with a real river, there's the need to really see what's what before leaping in and fishing. It was obvious that the water ran considerably higher when the turbines were on, so I began looking for pockets that would hold fish in these lower-water circumstances. It didn't take long. There were a series of gravel bars extending across the currents, gently sloping on the upstream sides, and cut sharply on the downstream side. The water on the downstream side was deep enough I couldn't see bottom. These pockets below the gravel bars had to be the concentrators.

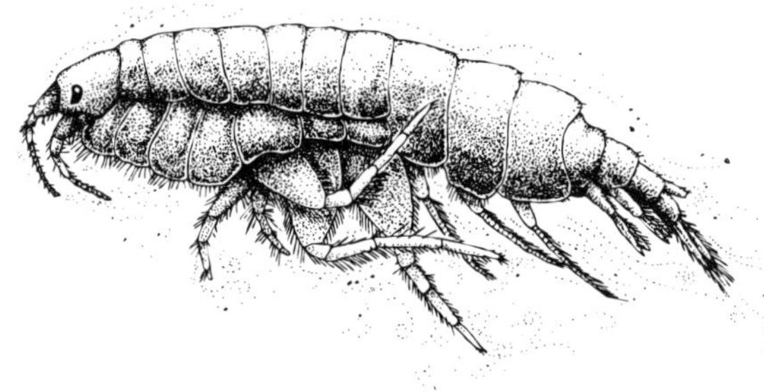

What to use? Again only a few moments of picking up rocks convinced me that the river was swarming with scuds. So, on the tippet went a size 12, gray, Hair Leg Scud and a small split shot (about a foot above the fly). All my calculations proved to be right, and a few casts later I had a nice rainbow. As I fished the pockets, I tried a variety of tactics, taking the odd fish, until I tried casting downstream and slowly and gently drawing the fly back upstream over the lip of the gravel bar. Suddenly I was into all sorts of fish.

When one fishes so close to the dam on tailwaters like the White, you're told to put a hundred dollar bill on a nearby rock. When the bill starts to float, grab it and run for the shore. If it's a hundred dollars, you won't take your eyes off it for more than a few seconds at a time. So, right in the middle of landing a nice rainbow, the warning siren on the dam went off. I simply dragged the fish after me as I headed to shore. Yes, the water does come up really fast!

Anglers that fish the White regularly know that downstream, as the waters begin to rise and flush out food items from the bottom, the fishing can be be exceptional. They will rush ahead of the moving water, get in position, fish the 20-minute to half-hour "hot time," then jump in the car and head to the next spot. It's an unusual kind of fishing, but reading waters is not just finding fish.

The San Juan

The San Juan is the child of the Navajo Dam near Farmington, New Mexico. As a tailwater fishery, it offers the fly fisher all the opportunities of a giant spring creek. It has shallows, islands, deep runs, monster pools, and very cold water. Nancy and Jason and I first fished the San Juan with Bob and Beverly Pelzl after one of our fly fishing schools at the Vermejo Ranch. The following story about that time is from my 1991 book, *Designing Trout Flies*:

> "We'll fish worms;" Bob told me, "the big trout of the San Juan can't resist them." I was silent in disbelief, surely Bob knew that I preferred to fly fish. And, I thought, he too had long since given up fishing with bait. Bob held out a closed hand. "Here's your bait." As I opened my mouth to decline, he opened his hand to reveal a cluster of orange and red flies of unique design tied on 3XL hooks. "We call them the San Juan Worm," he laughed. "Had you going didn't I"? I vaguely remember mumbling something about Bob's ancestry.
>
> It was early morning in August of 1976, and we were nearly to the pools that Bob had described. Mist rose from the water into the cold air of the high desert dawn, and the down vest and chamois shirt felt good. As we waded into the stream at the "log run," I was startled by its chill. The thermometer registered 44 degrees F. While I rigged my rod and threaded a strike indicator onto the leader, Bob explained, "The discovery was an accident. Jim Aubrey and I were fishing here a couple of years ago, and this fly, which was designed as a shrimp pattern for alpine lakes, really worked. Our subsequent investigation revealed a population of aquatic worms living in the silt of the river's bottom, and this fly turned out to be a pretty good imitation. You'll have to give Jim a hard time about it, though, he still refuses to call his fly a 'worm.'"
>
> Worm fly or not, the silver-bright rainbows of the river loved it. The take was never gentle; the indicator would leap upstream as the fish grabbed the fly and dashed away over the stony bottom or cartwheeled into the rapidly warming air.
>
> It was fishing of such quality that only when the feeding slowed did we realize how hot the August day had become. As we drove back to the temperature-controlled environment of our motel room at "Abes," I sat quietly, thinking of the stark beauty of the arid landscape and the magnificent fishery, where for the first time since childhood, I'd caught trout on worms.
>
> Bob and I keyed the worms and discovered that they were truly aquatic, not earthworms that had simply fallen or been washed into the river. These aquatic annelids belong to the family *Lumbriculidae*. They live in the sand and silts of the river bottom, and are especially abundant in tailwater fisheries and spring creeks.

When Bob and I first fished "The Worm," we concentrated on the smaller side channels and runs where the fishing is a bit more intimate; where one can wade and fish the Shotgun Tactic or a modified Leisenring Lift with ease. But as I used the fly on rivers like the Bighorn and Bow, I found that it works anywhere one can get a good dead-drift with it, regardless of the river's size. There are huge pools on those rivers, where I've taken nice fish right at the top lip, just like fishing smaller streams; side currents, like "G Run" on the Bow; rapids, (like those on the 'horn), and other places. The trick to fishing this fly is to get it in the water. Then, if one selects the prime lies and gets it in there, the catch rate goes up even more; river size is immaterial.

Below: A nice San Juan rainbow with Jim Aubrey's original "worm" firmly in place.

Lakes & Ocean Flats

There's more to reading lakes and ocean flats than I can possibly hope to cover in a single chapter; however, I can certainly spell out the major concepts which will allow the fly fisher to find fish and begin a deeper study of these waters. It may seem strange to mix a bit of salty brine in with the whole of lakes, but the reality of it is, they are quite similar in our basic understanding of reading waters.

Lakes

A lake is defined as a body of water contained in a basin. Remember, a stream is a body of flowing water contained in a channel. Now comes the fun part. There are "lakes" that are parts of stream systems. For example, a stream may open up into a shallow area and form a large pool of water that seems to be "lake-like," and hence receives the lake nomenclature. And then there's pond versus lake. How big does a pond have to be to become a lake? And what about stock tanks, are they not really ponds? Of course there are man-made lakes that are created by damming rivers. These are reservoirs, unless you are an engineer, then the reservoir is the "pool." One can't even really define a "basin," because it can be elongate, rounded, deep, shallow, etc. About the only thing that can be said is that the majority of the water in a lake has no unidirectional flow, as is characteristic of a stream. No wonder this lake fishing thing can get a bit confusing. Let's just say that we all have a mental image of "lake" versus "stream," and go from there, making some notes on exceptions as we go along.

Water Colors

Understanding how light moves through lake waters is important because fish will move from deep to shallow waters much more quickly in stillwaters than in streams. Light transmission can have an very definite effect on the flies and tactics used as the angler follows feeding fish when they are changing depths. Not only do different food organisms occupy different depth, but line density will play an important role is getting the flies to the correct feeding zone.

Thus it is that one of the ways in which the water in lakes can be classified is by the clarity of the water. Pure water seems, of course, very nearly "transparent" to light. That is, it seems to have very little resistance to the passage of light through it. So, water of any other "color" is water with something in it. That something can vary from algae, to partly dissolved organic matter, to tannins, to silt and clay particles. All of these influence the transmission of light through the water, both vertically and horizontally. And actually, water, itself, does absorb and scatter light. Clean lakes look blue, like the sky, because they scatter blue light the most.

The vertical transmission of light is an interesting phenomenon. Clear water absorbs specific colors of the light spectrum differentially. The spectrum of white light can be broken down into red, orange, yellow, green, blue, indigo, and violet components (a rainbow, for example). Clear fersh water absorbs these colors in that same sequence: red is completely absorbed by 6 feet down; orange by 15 feet; yellow by 21 feet; green by 27 feet; the blues by 30 feet. Thus, a red fly will appear a shade of gray below about 6 feet unless it is a color of red that has a little orange in it, and so on.

Now comes the fun part. When water contains algae or tannins it absorbs the various wavelengths of light differently than clean water. In water with a significant amount of algae, both the red and the blue are all gone by 6 feet down; this is because the plants use red and blue light for photosynthesis. All the other wavelengths are absorbed basically the same as light in clear water. In a bog lake, with a high tannin content, all the light is basically absorbed by 10 feet down. Red makes it to 6 feet; orange, yellow, and green get to 10 feet; and blue only makes it to 4 feet. This can have real significance if one is attempting to present a specific color at a depth below its threshold depth. Fluorescent materials, however, retain their colors as long as there's light, black is always black, and flash is always flash.

Then, there's the whole issue of background space light. This is the color of the water as it appears when looking around underwater in a horizontal direction. In clear water at a depth less than 6 feet, the water appears a light, silvery blue. The deeper one gets the darker this coloration becomes. Background space light is caused by the scattering (not absorption) of light rays, and blue is scattered more than other colors. Near the surface in waters with algae, the background space light is pale yellowy green, growing darker with depth. Algae absorb the blue and red wavelengths very strongly, allowing the green and yellow colors to become prominent. In bog waters, the background space light near the surface is light reddish brown, obviously getting darker as one goes deeper. Tannins in the water absorb blue light very strongly, allowing the reds and greens to show through. Red and green make brown.

Background space light only adds more complications to the overall picture. Suddenly, one has to design flies according to the color of the water in which they are to be fished. Well, there is some truth to that if one wants to accent a color or design an attractor fly with an emphasized color. But if the imitation matches the color of the natural, then the fish will see it in the same light as the natural (yes, a pun and not a pun). As noted earlier, fluorescent colors don't change, black is black, and flash is flash.

Color vision in fish is a response to background space light. A color-blind fish would only see in shades of gray (called the "gray level"). So if a food organism had the same gray level as the background space light, it would be essentially invisible to the fish. Color vision allows the fish to differentiate food organisms by their hue (specific color), their chroma (intensity of color or color saturation), and by their gray level. Some fish have developed UV vision, allowing them to see beyond the blue range and into the near ultra-violet, detecting "colors" that to us are black. Certainly color detection is not the only way fish sense prey, but it certainly helps.

The fish's eye is well adapted to its life underwater and is equipped with color vision to discern prey against background space light.

Water Depth

Water depth is the single factor with the greatest effect on the fish's position in lakes. That's a rather bold statement, but true, none-the-less. Depth influences plant growth, light levels, temperature, oxygen levels, food abundance, and overhead cover, and fish are sensitive to all of these. So, let's get it straight, right up front: for the serious lake angler, a depth finder (fish locator) is a smart tool to have. Not something that the big charter captains use out in 200 fathoms, but an easily managed tool that allows the angler to quickly locate those depths at which fish are holding at any given time. Yes there are exceptions, and I'll get into these in a bit, but for now, we need to deal with the need to locate fish in a broad body of water where there's no ability to read the bottom by looking at the top or surrounding terrain.

I was speaking in Oregon one spring, and Fred Foisset, who owns and operates Cascade Guides & Outfitters in Sun River, took a day off to fish Big Lava Lake with my friend, Marc Williamson, and me. Fred fishes all the lakes in the Bend, Oregon area, and knows them very well. Even with that extensive knowledge, he leans on his locator very heavily. He might know the bottom structures of the lakes, but he doesn't know which one the fish have chosen on any particular day. There are too many variables to consider when searching every possible bottom structure, so he grabs the locator and finds the fish, right now.

As soon as we left the dock, Fred noted a significant number of fish holding along a submerged line of weeds about 20 feet down. We made a mental note and went on. Up toward the far end of the lake there was an underwater drop off that Fred wanted to explore. Sure enough, there were fish on the ledge about 12 feet down. These were easier to reach than those 20 feet down, and so we rigged up intermediate lines and small, weighted leeches. The trick was to feed out the entire line and drift over the drop off at the right speed.

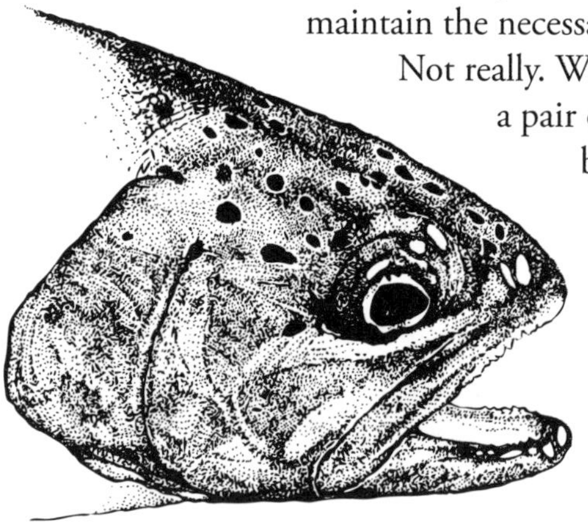

That meant using a sea anchor (an underwater drogue chute) to maintain the necessary slow drift of the boat. Sound complicated? Not really. Well, maybe a bit more involved than tossing on a pair of waders and heading off to the local stream, but not that much more complicated. We just used a sea anchor, and didn't have to put the waders on. Whenever we passed over the ledge, one, two, and sometimes all three of us hooked up on a rainbow. I wish I could report that they were all monsters, but they weren't No monsters at all that day, nothing but constant action, good company, and beautiful mountain scenery.

Later in the afternoon, as the day warmed, we drifted back over to the area near the dock and found the fleet of fish had move up to between 10 and 12 feet. So we had at them the same way as we fished those on the ledge. Without the locator we might have caught the same number that we saw others catching—an occasional fish, or no fish.

But wait, you say, I don't use a boat, I only fish from a float-tube. Well, that's okay on smaller waters or on big waters if using a tender boat, but there's still no reason not to have a depth indicator. They come in all sizes and strengths with nearly every bell and whistle that anyone could ever need, including one that uses a remote transducer and can be hand held.

I'm not trying to dictate to anyone regarding gear, and if you fish ponds or small to medium-sized lakes that you know very well and have figured out completely, then obviously leave the locator at home. Or, if you just love the adventure of exploring and sussing out fish locations, then by all means do so. This is our sport to enjoy as we please. So, please enjoy it to its fullest in the way that is most gratifying to you.

Intimate knowledge of smaller waters allows the angler to zoom in on the fish under all conditions.

Having said all that, let me point out that Nancy and Jason and I spent over 20 years teaching fly fishing schools on the Vermejo Ranch in northeast New Mexico. There are 20-plus trout lakes on the property, and we fished them all intensely. We did map a couple of the deeper lakes with a locator, but after that we didn't use one. There were 10 reasons: (1) Once we really knew the lakes we knew where the fish would be during the time we were there. (2) The lakes have absolutely classic weed beds with both floating and submerged beds. (3) There are perfect inshore cruising zones between the weed beds and the shoreline. (4) The trout were active cruisers. (5) The damselflies were hatching in the time that we selected for the schools. The nymphs swim to shore to emerge, so we knew this would enhance the number of cruisers. (6) We discovered the first year that when the fish weren't using the inshore cruising lanes, they were out over the submerged weed beds. (7) The fish rose freely for every hatching and egg laying session, damelfies, caddises, midges, and mayflies. (8) The elevation of the lakes was high enough to keep the inshore waters cool throughout the day. (9) There were plenty of mountain "breezes" to keep the lakes highly oxygenated. (10) I like hunting cruisers more than any other kind of fishing.

So, our knowledge of these lakes, combined with constant input from the biologists at the ranch and other angling guests, kept us on top of the fishing every moment. That, however, is not always the case, as in the fishing that I did with Marc and Fred. So, the fishing in small, intimate lakes can be figured out with a season or two of experience. But in new lakes, and/or big lakes, a locator can be the ideal tool to get into fish quickly.

In the Zone

Water depth is the key to weed growth in lakes, and weed beds are always fish magnets. The weeds feed the bugs that feed the fish; weeds provide cover for the fish; and weed beds are areas high in oxygen. When one examines a lake from the standpoint of depth and weed growth, there are **three distinct "zones"** that can be identified: The **littoral zone**, **limnetc zone**, and **profundal zone** *(Figure 10.1)*.

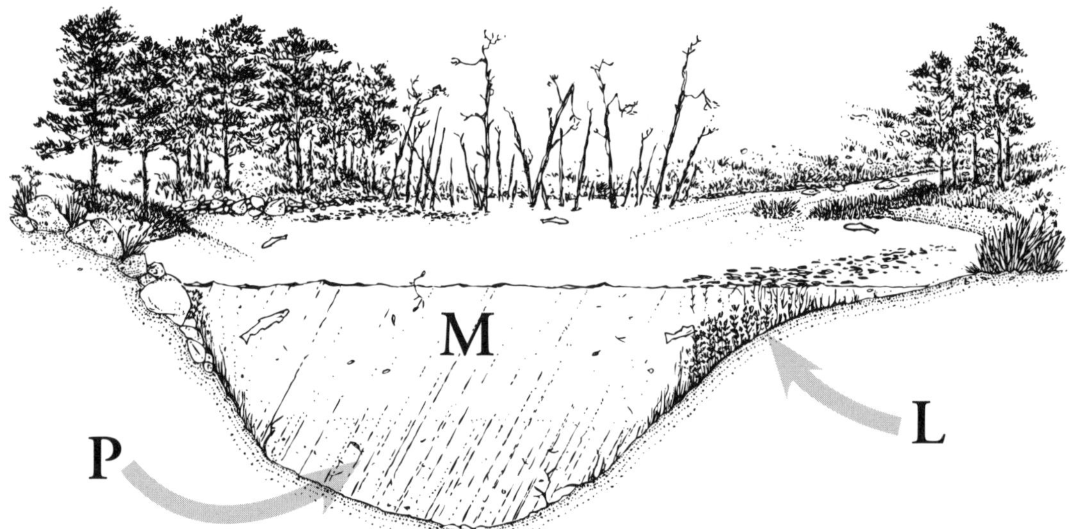

Figure 10.1. *Stillwaters can be divided into three general zones: the littoral (L), the limnetic (M), and the profundal (P).*

The littoral zone is that near-shore area in which rooted plants can grow. Typically this is in water less than 30 feet deep. If the entire lake is less than 30 feet deep, the whole thing can be one giant littoral zone. Henry's Lake in Idaho is just such a lake. Its abundant fish population and the large average size of the fish are a direct result of the super-abundance of weeds with the subsequent super-abundance of food. In deeper lakes, the littoral zone forms a "ring around the lake." And, as one would suspect, in shallower areas it will extend much farther out from shore than in areas where the bottom drops off sharply. Furthermore, in larger lakes there is often an open-water "cruising zone" next to shore where wave action keeps the weeds from taking root.

In lakes, fish swim, or cruise, about looking for food rather than holding in a lie. Thus in lakes, one looks for "cruising lanes" rather than lies, when searching for fish in non-hatch times. Even in times of heavy insect activity, many fish will use the cruising lanes. Anything in the lake that can be defined as an "edge" can form a cruising lane: the edge of a delta, a weed edge, either along floating plants or over submerged ones, around flooded timber or big boulders, along a deep water drop off, an old stream channel, and so on. Open water "pockets" in beds of emergent or floating-leaf plants are also great spots to find fish.

While Jason and I have fished many lakes, from small ponds to the Great Lakes, our favorite style of lake fishing is hunting cruisers. No waders, usually. The idea is to walk the bank, very slowly, and watch for cruisers. They are normally quite spooky and require careful stalking and equally careful casting. We use every spot of cover that we can, hiding behind or in front of vegetation, trees, boulders, irregularities in the ground, and so on. The fish are often so close that it's necessary to use a Bow and Arrow Cast to flip the fly in front of them without having to raise the rod and most likely spook the fish. To see a nice rainbow or brown fin up to a tiny dry and carefully inspect it before gently sipping it in is heart-stopping excitement. It gets in one's blood.

A few years back, Jason and his wife, Kelley, were fishing a lake with some big cruisers working in front of them. Kelley was fishing and Jason was playing "gillie." A brown trout unexpectedly eased out of the weeds only a few feet away. Kelley held motionless while Jason started shooting photos to document the event. The fish turned and started to move away. With a tiny flick, Kelley dropped the little dry a few feet out from the fish. It moved over immediately and sucked in the imitation. It literally splashed water on her when she set the hook, it was that close.

Kelley staying motionless as the "unexpected brown" turns back out along the weed edge. This fish actually fed on the surface among the rocks just out from Kelley's feet.

In a typical lake, one can expect to find emergent vegetation close to shore. If there is a strong wave zone or cruising zone next to shore, then the emergent plants will be at the outside edge of it. These are plants like reeds and cattails that literally "emerge" above the surface. Next is an area of floating-leaf plants like lily pads or pondweed. At the outside depth of the floating-leaf plants come the submerged weed beds. These cover the bottom out to about 30 feet in depth (for clear lakes). Beyond that there are no rooted plants. Thus the littoral zone is "littered" with aquatic plants. Don't expect to find this exact sequence of plants in every lake you fish, nor in every area of every lake you fish.

For example, Adams Lake on the Vermejo Ranch has a gently sloping, shallow-water eastern shore. There's a cruising zone 15 to 50 feet wide, then tall rushes in patches, then floating pondweed, and finally, submerged weeds that run on out to 100 feet or more from shore. The north shore lies against a steep rocky bank, and the cruising lane is 15 feet at its widest. There are only a few areas with pondweed, and no rushes. One can stand on the hillside and see the outer edge of the submerged weeds. The west shore is similar to the north shore. But then at the southwest corner, a feeder from Leandro Creek has created a delta, and there are again rushes and pondweed. This delta blends into a shallow bay that is reflected in the gently sloping topography of the valley that lies off to the southwest of the lake. The south shore is a repeat of the north shore. Thus, one can find all the variations in the littoral zone in a simple walk around the lake.

Top: An example of a Vermejo lake showing a gradual slope of land that gently projects into the water. In this case, it provides a broad cruising area for trout.

Bottom: The steep north shore of Adams Lake drops off sharply and the weed beds are in quite close (in some cases completely tight to the shoreline).

Each area fishes differently. It's not at all unusual to find fish feeding both on the surface and several feet down over the sunken weed beds on both the gently sloping eastern and southwestern shores. The cruiser fishing can be phenomenal in both these areas because of the wide cruising zone—lots of fish moving back and forth looking for food in water that is inches to a couple of feet deep. The other shore areas have cruisers, but they are in close, and can move to deep water almost instantly. There are fewer fish, overall, because the cruising zone is very narrow in many places. There are certainly fish feeding several feet down along the tops of the submerged vegetation, but again, the plants don't extend more than about 50 feet out into the lake, limiting the submerged-weed-bed zone where fish can feed.

One of the things that is common on all lakes, is that the terrain of the shoreline often projects the terrain of the lake bottom, usually as far as the outer edge of the littoral zone. A steep bank on shore translates as a steep drop into the lake. A gentle slope of the land into the lake translates into a gentle slope of the bottom. A cliff above water equals a cliff below water, and so on. Of course, there are exceptions, but as a general rule, reading the land forms around the lake allows the angler to read the waters of the lake—usually as far out as the deep edge of the littoral zone.

And it's the littoral zone that one wants to watch first and foremost. Even if the water is a bit on the warm side, trout will move into the littoral zone and feed if there are heavy insect hatches. To help see what's going on, I carry a small pair of binoculars that allow me to scan areas that are too far away to see with the unaided eye.

One spring I was invited to Spokane, Washington, to present a seminar, and afterward, a number of club members took me fishing on Dry Falls Lake. It's an amazing geological feature. Part of the Columbia River of the past, it is actually the plunge pool of an enormous waterfall that was 400 feet high and 3 ½ miles across. There's a tourist turnout on the road that runs along the rim with the usual set of "pay to see" binoculars that allow one to better view the features pointed out on the adjacent placard. I looked through them at the shallow end of the lake.

"Do you guys hunt those cruisers?" I asked.

"What cruisers?" Came the reply.

I knew it was going to be a really good day.

We drove down the side road to the lake edge, and I rigged up my rod and shouldered into my vest. I tied on a snail fly as we headed for the shallow bay where the fish were swimming about in search of food. I stalked slowly up to the edge and watched. There were several fish within casting distance, so I just picked the nearest one, and threw the fly about 10 feet ahead of it. It surged forward,

The snail fly can be to the stillwater angler what the Adams is to the stream angler—an all-around great pattern.

grabbed the fly, and then kept right on going as the hook went home. After the second fish in as many casts, I was "forced" to unload all my snail flies to the other anglers, but little matter. The guys had tying gear along, and snails are easy to tie.

There will be a complete discussion of all the lake's food organisms and fishing tactics in our upcoming book, *Stillwaters*.

Streams Under, In, and Out

For lakes that have been formed by damming streams, there will be an old stream channel in the bottom of the lake. This can be a superb place to find cruising fish. They will work the edges of the channel, especially during the bright light of the day when there are no hatches to move them out into other areas of the lake. So, knowing where the channel is can be a great help in finding fish. A good map of the lake can be very helpful in finding such features, as can a fish locator that reads bottom structure. Dry years, or at other times when impoundments are drawn down, offer the angler excellent opportunities for locating the position of normally submerged stream channels. (A few photos taken when the water is low can be an immense help when water levels return to normal.)

Some years back, our late friends, Phil and Barbara Clarke, had invited Nancy and me to fish with them at the Coleman Lake Club in northern Wisconsin. It was a lovely fall day, and Nancy had gone for a walk in the woods with our dog. Phil and Barbara and I pushed the wooden pram out into Railroad Pond and quietly rowed toward the upper end.

"The stream channel comes right around that stump and cuts across just in front of us," Phil told me. "We marked it with those dead branches."

I pitched the sinking line and Strip Leech about 50 feet up the channel and waited 15 seconds for it to sink. The take was far stronger than I expected, and as the rod tip snapped down hard, the 3X tippet parted. Duly chastened by my inattentiveness, I sheepishly replaced the fly and repeated the cast. This time I was ready when a hefty rainbow scooped up the undulating leech. And so it went; the old stream channel was full of fish and our probing flies took them with regularity.

The rainbows were patrolling the submerged stream channel and took the fly solidly.

Of course, a stream mouth as it enters a lake is always a superb spot to look for feeding fish. They will often move out of the lake proper and feed in the currents that spread out into the "stillwaters" of the lake.

On another occasion with Phil and Barbara Clarke, Nancy and I were fishing Brock Pond. Phil and I rowed up into the mouth of the Pike River while Barbara and Nancy fished the stream channel in the main lake. Phil and I found a cornucopia of fish parked up in the shallow water where the stream had dumped its load of sand and silt over the years. They were nice fish, up to about 15 inches, and we were more than happy to feed them our flies on a regular basis. Then, we came to a deeper area, near a large boulder, and I shot a nymph up into the head of the deep water and slowly began working it back. The strike was sudden and hard, and the fish certainly felt bigger than anything we'd taken that morning. Finally to boat, it proved to be a 23-inch rainbow, the biggest anyone had seen that season. It's always a good idea to spend some time in the *boca*.

Streams entering a lake deposit alluvial materials there, and can create some excellent cruising flats. In New Zealand, for example, there are truly large cruising flats at the top ends of lakes like Ohau, Wanaka, Hawea, and many others. There, one can find big fish searching for breakfast or dinner in the skinny water. They are extraordinarily spooky, and really take off when they're hooked. They don't wallow about, they just blast off like a rocket, heading the half-mile or so to deep water. The trick for these fish is to cast well ahead of them (as in 15 or more feet) and just let the fly sit still. If it's a dry that you're plying, then it's the old Heave-and-Leave—toss the fly out and do nothing else except wait for the snout to poke out and eat it. If it's a nymph, then use the Jumping Nymph Tactic. Let the fly settle to the bottom, and when the fish gets close, give it a short, quick jerk to pop it off the bottom and move it a few inches. If you're unsure of a take, then strip the line a bit. If it feels heavy, it is; a fish is holding the fly in its mouth. It's called "feeling for the fish."

Feeder streams also serve as spawning grounds for lake-bound fish, and during the run, there can be some extremely exciting fishing. The fall run of browns up the Madison River from Hebgen Lake is world renowned, and the fall runs of king and coho salmon and big browns and spring steelhead into the tributaries of the Great Lakes have to be seen to be fully comprehended. There are many such places where knowledgeable anglers can seek out such fishing.

Streams can also carry large amounts of flotsam into the lake during high water flows. Such debris, built up along a deep shoreline, will offer cover for any fish species, and are places that the angler should probe thoroughly.

Below: A Strip Nymph.

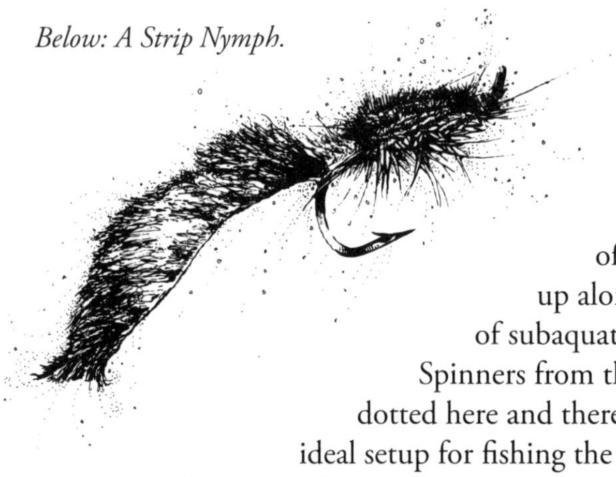

One June morning, quite early, on another visit to Coleman Lake Club, Phil and Barbara Clarke and Nancy and I pushed two boats out into the mist on Railroad Pond. Massive stumps of long-since-cut white pines had piled up along the shore, and expansive beds of subaquatic plants crowded against them. Spinners from the previous night's Hex activity were dotted here and there on the lake's gentle swells; it was the ideal setup for fishing the Strip Nymph. We knotted them to our leaders, and casting tight against the stumps, worked the imitations back over the sunken weeds. It was the right fly in the right place at the right time. The big rainbows and browns came to the fly like kids to candy.

The channel where a stream leaves a lake can also be a hot zone. One summer, Jason and I walked into Grebe Lake in Yellowstone Park with Jim Aubrey, Bob Pelzl, and Royce Dam. We were intending to fish for the big rainbows of the lake, but the day turned ugly. A raw north wind clawed at us, and the angry sky spit down a mix of snow and freezing-cold rain. We hiked around the rim of the lake to the outfall of the Gibbon River, and began fishing the waters of the lake just as they gathered into the stream channel. The total lack of surface activity—which would be expected in the frigid conditions we were experiencing—caused us to replace the floating lines on our reels with the spare spools of sinking lines we had carried in our vests.

The deep-water fishing proved to be quite good. We used gray scud imitations, and fished them with a slow hand-twist retrieve in the gathering currents. There were no rainbows in the outlet, but there were grayling, and we caught many of them. They were Jason's first grayling, and he worked at them tirelessly, cold fingers seemingly forgotten.

Find the Food, Find the Fish

Fish follow food, in lakes most especially. They can go from the shallows to the deep, literally in a matter of minutes. Many times, when fishing a damsel hatch, the trout will be practically on shore, feeding on the migrating insects. When the nymphs cease their swimming for the day, the in-shore cruising zone can empty out so fast you'll wonder if there are any fish in the lake. They don't stay to hunt for food if there's no food to hunt.

They've gone in search of other cruising areas where food is plentiful. Find the food, and you'll find the fish.

One summer, on a busman's holiday from our fly fishing schools on the Vermejo Ranch, all the instructors were fishing Number One Lake, high on the shoulders of the *Sangre de Cristo* Mountains. All of us were hammering the big rainbows with damsel nymphs from the moment we arrived until just before noon. Then the fish just stopped. The nymphal migration was over. We headed back to the vehicle and grabbed the picnic boxes. It was a warm pleasant day, and I decided that a little after-lunch nap was in order. Just a small one, mind you.

As I settled in, Bob Pelzl and Jim Aubrey pushed a boat out onto the lake and rigged up their sinking lines. Before I could even get my eyes closed, they were into fish—on every cast. On the first cast, Bob had counted to 15 before retrieving the line; Jim had counted to 20. Bob caught a fish; Jim caught the weeds. On the next cast, they both counted to 15, and both caught fish. Then they began playing "musical flies." Every time one of them caught a fish, they had to tie on a different fly. Well, they even tied on dry flies and fished them at 15 counts down, and still caught fish. The trout weren't selective to the fly, they were selective to the depth. They were cruising about eight feet down over a submerged weed bed and feeding actively.

No matter what fly Bob and Jim used, they took trout as long as they fished at the proper depth.

British anglers that regularly ply the reservoirs of that country have become masters of following the movements of the fish as they seek different depths in search of food. They will often carry multiple rods, each rigged with a different line density and fly type. In early morning they often fish with a floating line and midge emerger or adult pattern.

As the sun creeps up, they switch to an intermediate line and a fly like a midge pupa. By 9 am, they'll be using a type 1 sinking line and damsel nymph or perhaps a snail fly down five or six feet over sunken weeds. By 11 am, they've got the type 2 sinker on, and are working deeper weeds with a fluorescent red minnow imitations or perhaps a big dragonfly nymph. After lunch, they'll switch to a type 3 sinking line and maybe tie on a blood worm larva to fish along the bottom in open waters just beyond the littoral zone. About five in the afternoon, they begin to rotate back up through the lines until at dark, they're back up on top. It's an effective tactic.

Open Waters

Out beyond the littoral zone is open water that we can separate into the upper, lighted portion (down to about 30 feet in clear lakes) called the limnetic zone (limnos = lake), and the deep, dark portion of the lake called the profundal zone (profound = deep) (see *Figure 10.1*). These are areas that should not be neglected. In fact, many anglers think that all the fish in the lake live in this, the deepest part of the lake. Well, that's certainly seems a logical place if they're all trying to hide, but largely, fish spend most of their time in and near the littoral zone. However, since fish follow food, if there's food out in the open water, there will be fish out there eating.

A great example of this goes back to the mid-1980s when a group of us were fishing a Rocky Mountain high-country lake. True to form, I found a spot for a short siesta in the shade of a big ponderosa pine. In fact, all of us were taking a siesta. As I lay there, more half asleep than half awake, I heard a "plop," and then another. It sounded like fish rising. I tipped my Stetson up and looked out onto a lake riddled with rising fish.

The siesta was over in a heartbeat. We bolted to our boats and rowed out into the open water beyond the littoral zone. There were fish rising everywhere. A quick examination of the water showed that it was covered with leafhoppers, carried there from the nearby forest lands by the wind. It was an unforgettable day's fishing, to put it directly.

On other occassions we've encountered ant-falls that strain credibility. How there can be that many insects in the land around the lake is just baffling, but there they are on the water, with fish eating them without caution—until one tries to catch those fish. Then, they're closed mouth. The trick, we've discovered, is to cast four to six feet ahead of a fish, move the fly just a tiny bit, and then let it lie still. This movement causes the fish to notice the fly, and then, often move to take it amidst the scores of naturals.

Hatches of aquatic insects—mayflies, caddises, and midges, often occur on the outer edges of the littoral zone, and the emergers and adults can get blown out into the open water beyond. This can create some significant angling opportunities.

Duane Stremlau and I had gone to fish the Madison Arm of Hebgen Lake and found ourselves right in the middle of a heavy *Callibaetis* hatch. The Speckled Wing Duns were being blown out into open water, and the fish went after them. We went after the fish in our float-tubes. The fishing was good, but it was the *looong* paddle back to shore when the hatch was over that I remember the most. Next time I'll remember to paddle back upwind every half hour or so and run through the drift again.

"Late to bed and early to rise" is a good motto to have if you want to hit the best angling times in most stillwaters.

There's the old angler's adage that the best times to fish are morning and evening, and that can certainly be the case if no other over-riding factors, like mid-day hatches, are in play. There are two main reason: (1) the lower light levels at that time of day make the fish feel less fearful of the surface and of shallow water, and (2) there is a diurnal movement of micro-crustacean food organisms such as the water flea (*Daphnia*) from the bottom to the surface at dusk, and a return of these food organisms to the bottom in the dawn. Small fish and predatory insects feeding on these zooplankters, in turn, attract larger fish to feed on them.

Lakes and Winds

There's not been a lake made that doesn't have wind blowing across it—and always in the opposite direction that one needs to row or paddle. Wind and waves are just a matter of life on lakes, and the fly fisher who is serious about lake fishing will have to learn to deal with head winds, crossing winds, and tailing winds. Many lake anglers have gone to intermediate lines for fishing dry flies because the thinner diameter of the line allows it to knife through the wind more easily. Just dress the line heavily with fly floatant to keep it as much on top as possible. Fishing an intermediate is about the closest thing the modern-day angler has to fishing a silk line (unless, of course, one actually does fish a silk line).

But, the wind can be the fly fisher's friend, too. If there are waves, I will use them to help activate a nymph, snail fly, small leech, and so on. I use a larger foam indicator up on the leader a foot or three, and then cast into the area where I suspect fish are cruising.

The indicator rides up and down on the waves, causing the fly to jig up and down. This "Wave Bobbing Tactic" has been very effective for me in many places. If I can, I like to cast across the wind. First, it's easier to cast across wind than into the wind or with a following wind. Second, the angler can cover the water more effectively when casting in the across wind direction.

And don't think that waves put fish down. Often, it stimulates them into feeding mode. The waves whip oxygen into the water, stir up the weeds, and displace food organisms, lifting them up into the open water over the weeds and into the cruising zone next to shore. This is often a great time to fish a snail fly. The mollusks are swept off the weeds by the waves, and are drifting about in the waters above. I've had many days of great fishing with all manner of nymph, pupa, leech, snail, and adult imitations when the wind was whipping, but there's one day that truly stands above all the others.

We were fishing Vermejo's Adams Lake in anticipation of a hatch of the Giant Traveling Sedge (*Banksiola crotchi*). We knew they would hatch in great numbers in late afternoon, and Bob Pelzl and I were sitting under the trees on the lake's north side waiting on the hatch. Suddenly, we heard the sound of distant wind. At first, we didn't know where it was, but then we saw the trees on the opposite shore bow their heads to the tempest roaring in off the peaks to the south. The lake whipped into "white horses" in a heartbeat, and with the big waves came the hatch. It was not the hatch we were expecting, but a hatch of heart-stopping enormity. The caddis were running up over the waves, running across the face of the waves, surfing the waves—they were everywhere. The waves were so large that we could look right into their faces and see trout everywhere. They were rushing around, anxiously trying to grab every caddis they could find.

It was almost weird fishing into the faces of the waves to these wild-eyed rainbows. They would blow right out of the face of a wave and nail the Devil Bug that was sliding down the curl. We only had to cast 15 to 20 feet, and that was good, considering the wind we were casting into. We didn't have to use light tippets, either. The fish took the fly willingly on 2X, so our landing tactic could more rightly called "dragging" than fighting. We were as anxious to catch the trout as the trout were to catch the caddis.

Our Devil Bugs didn't have to go far to find fish feeding in the waves.

A constant and significant wind will set up wind lanes. As the wind blows along the surface, it sets up water circulation vortices in which the currents are perpendicular to the direction of the wind. The line where two adjacent vortices intersect is a wind lane *(Figure 10.2)*. One can see foam lines in these wind lanes, and if the foam builds up, food builds up, and fish build up. These wind lanes may remain in place for a couple of days after a period of strong wind, and savvy anglers will be fishing the foam.

Figure 10.2. *A long wind lane or "scum line." This one is on Montana's Quake Lake.*

Wind on a lake can also be good for Blow-line fishing. One needs a little wind, but not a gale. The line is 8 to 15 feet of polypropylene fly tying yarn. It's an untwisted yarn that allows the wind to really catch it. One end is tied to the butt of the leader and a tippet is added to the other end. The angler then holds the rod up and allows the wind to dance the fly over the surface of the water. The take can be rather violent. This is a slick tactic for adult caddises and damselflies. See our book, *Fishing the Film,* for more details on this approach.

Ocean Flats

While this book has been focused more on freshwater, everything that I've discussed about fishing lake flats applies to fishing ocean flats. There are some considerations in ocean flats fishing, however, that lake fishers never have to think about. The most prominent of these is the tide; then there are sharks, and rays, and barracuda, and coral, and shells, and mangroves and....

The tide is the single over-riding factor in finding fish on the flats. The fish follow the tide in and follow the tide out. As the tide moves in, the flats come alive, and the fish find ample food to eat. Then as the tide slides out, the fish go with it. So, flats fishers time their excursions to the tides. There are two high tides and two low tides a day, about six hours apart. What I always hope for is an early morning and late afternoon incoming tide, and thereby get two good fishing periods in one day.

Ocean flats are similar to those on lakes, with the exceptions of the tide, sharks, barracuda, and a host of other species not present in fresh water.

Another major difference between fishing the lake flats for big cruising trout and fishing ocean flats is the presence of other fishes on the flats. These include sharks and sting rays that can pose a physical danger to the fly fisher. Sharks almost never present any real danger to a wading angler unless the fly fisher is dragging bloody fish, a bait bucket, or other shark-attractive items. Rays, on the other hand, do present a danger that fly fishers need to carefully avoid. Slide your feet a bit rather than lifting your feet and stepping down. Stepping down runs the risk of tromping on a ray and getting a stinger in the leg. It's not something that one has to be overly anxious about, just something that one needs to keep in the back of one's mind.

Flats in the ocean are as variable as flats in lakes. They can be bare or partially/fully covered with vegetation, they can have compacted or loose bottoms, they can have emergent reeds and brush, or not. They can be dry at low tide and flooded perfectly at high tide. Don't ever expect the same thing exactly the same way it was the last time, even on the same flat. Always approach any water—ocean flat, lake flat, riffle, pool, run, and so forth—as if it were a new, or at least freshened, place. Certainly, if it's a place that you fish often,

Mangrove edges are especially powerful fish magnets on ocean flats.

you will know many of the spots where fish feed, but fish seem to be designed to surprise the fly fisher, so always be watching.

Ocean flats are typically cut with channels, which are the main current feeders during incoming and outgoing tides. Fish ride the channels when moving onto and off the flats. Sometimes, one can have good fishing in the channels as the tide is sweeping in, but usually this is rather blind fishing. I prefer to wait until the fish get up on the flats and then stalk them individually.

If there are mangroves on the flats, then the fish will often move in and around them as they feed. Be especially alert in such areas because fish can suddenly appear as if from nowhere as they move out into open water from a clump of mangroves.

On the flats, one really has to learn to see fish. This is a mater of practice, but also a matter of understanding what to look for. The story, "First Bone" in Chapter One is a good example of spotting fish.

See the bonefi..., er, trout? A cruising fish, a sand flat, the same concepts. Spotting fish on any flat is a matter of knowing what to look for and how to look for it. Check out the fish's shape, its shadow, its surface disturbance, and its physical movement/flash (you'll have to imagine that last part). From farther away, the surface disturbance and shadow would be two big tip-offs, trout, bonefish, or otherwise. Note that this photo was taken with a polarizing filter (just like a good pair of polarizing glasses).

Watch, too, for shadows, the flash of a fish's side, "nervous" water, plumes of mud or sand kicked up by bottom feeding activity, and all other possible "out of place" movements and colors. Seeing fish is a matter of looking *into* the water and not just looking *at* the water, so concentrate on this skill. Also, like fishing for tigers in Africa, watching for the activity of birds is another salty reading trick that can be very important in certain circumstances (this is typically a more open-water aspect of reading). Be sure that you always wear your polarizing glasses to give yourself every advantage. And above all, don't hurry. Once you learn to see fish, your angling score will rise dramatically. There will be plenty of notes on seeing fish in our forthcoming book, *The Angler as Predator.*

Flats are broad areas with shallow water. The bottom is more-or-less "flat." And while fishing these is basically the same as fishing flats in lakes, there are plenty of other shore-line areas in the ocean that are not flats. First and foremost, when fishing the non-flats shoreline, look at its topography—gradually getting deeper, rapidly getting deeper, rocky, sandy, algae beds, coral reefs, and so on. Then read these areas just as you would similar lake areas. Edges are still the places of most interest.

In *Striper Strategies; Secrets of a Striper Bum*, my late friend, Jack Gartside, recommends that anyone fishing a new area stay through an entire tide cycle in order to get a good look at the bottom at both high and low tide. This allows the angler to best determine areas that fish are more prone to prowl at high tide. And even though high tide is usually the best fishing time, Jack notes that in marsh ponds, mid-tide can be great top-water time just a dawn and at dark.

Often, when bait gets in close to the shore, fish like stripers and bluefish can "blitz" them, forcing them right into the wave wash on the beach. When one encounters such an occurrence, the fishing can be hot and heavy. Other times the bait may stay out a bit, and you have to toss the imitation out beyond the second breaker or farther. This is the time of a shooting head and stripping basket, a stripping glove, and if the surf is up, full chest-high waders and the best rain jacket money can buy. Still, the chance of hooking a monster striper or blue keeps one casting no matter what the weather.

Then, too, there are large areas of coastal marshes where "ponds" are linked by interconnecting "rivers." Where stripers live, these places can be dynamite. They can also be as empty as a hobo's tin can. But when they're on, they're on. If such a "river" is a deep inlet or outlet to a marsh pond, it will likely hold fish at all times, but the time of tide changes can be especially productive as bait fish are swept into and out of the marshes. More specific information will be found in our forthcoming book, *Stillwaters.*

Whether it's finding fish on a tiny mountain stream, exploring the sweep of a huge river, or plotting to take cruising trout or bones, reading waters is a multi-faceted skill that leads the angler to life-long adventures in the waters of the world. It's one of nature's great texts that requires careful study, but which also offers great rewards.

Annotated Bibliography

Bashline, L James. 1973. Night Fishing for Trout. Freshet Press, Rockville Centre, NY. Purely devoted to night fishing, this is both an informative and fun book. Bashline grew up fishing some of the best night pools in America and rubbed shoulders with the best night fishers, becoming one himself.

Borger, Gary A. 1971. Nymphing. Stackpole Books, Harrisburg, PA. My first book with information on identifying naturals and tying, and fishing artificial nymphs.

Brooks, Charles E. 1972. The Trout and the Stream. Crown Publishers, Inc., New York, NY. A text by one of the best, no-nonsense, big-trout fishermen I've ever known. There's plenty of good solid information in this book, including a good look at his thoughts on reading water.

Brooks, Joe. 1972. Trout Fishing. Outdoor Life. New York, NY. A wrap up of all the really top-notch trout fishing info of the day and some forward looking thoughts that have only recently become part-and-parcel of the general fly fishing methodology. Truly a milestone text.

Dick, Lennox. 1966, 1972. The Art and Science of Fly Fishing. Citadel Press, Secaucus, NJ. Primarily a book on reading waters, Dick takes the fly fisher through the season explaining flies and tactics as they apply to specific water types.

Gartside, Jack. 1997, 2008. Striper Strategies; Secrets of a Striper Bum. Self Published. Jack was an extraordinarily observant angler, and he especially loved striper fishing. He could find them even when they supposedly weren't there. All his self-published texts are well-worth the read.

Hughes, Dave. Reading the Water. 1988. Stackpole Books, Harrisburg, PA. Dave is a good writer and knows his stuff. This book is a careful look at the whole of reading streams.

Knight, Richard Alden. 1968. Successful Trout Fishing. E.P. Dutton and Co., Inc., New York, NY. A really great book on fishing the dry fly down and across with action. In addition there are plenty of other excellent ideas and thoughts on the whole fly fishing process.

Koch, Ed. 1972. Fishing the Midge. Freshet Press, Rockville Centre, NY. A solid look at fishing the little stuff. Ed covers more than the midge insects, showing tactic and patterns.

Lawson, Mike. 2003. Spring Creeks. Stackpole Books, Harrisbirg, PA. A thorough look at spring creeks in both a vertical and horizontal fashion. Mike looks at his river, the Henry's Fork, through the lens of time and the work others have done on spring creeks, including those in England and across the U.S. This is a great book on tackle, techniques, and the whole development of modern emerger fishing.

Bios

About Gary

Fly fishing has been a part of my life since I was 10 years old, when I was introduced to the sport through stories in "Field and Stream," "True," "Outdoor Life," "Sports Afield," and other magazines of the era. I asked for a fly tying kit for my 11th Christmas, and began creating and fishing the most awful looking flies that ever came off a tyer's bench. But they were my flies, and they caught fish. No trout, mind you, but there were plenty of chubs and panfish around.

My first trout on a fly came in 1956, a few weeks before my 12th birthday. Though only 10 inches long—and probably stocked the week before—that rainbow has always been my most memorable "trophy." By age 16, I could hit the highways to more distant waters, and my tying and fishing skills fooled enough trout to keep me thoroughly engaged.

When I entered college at Penn State, I found fantastic fishing on Spring Creek, as well as a wonderful angling library sustained by the university's many fly-fishing faculty. In my junior year at Penn State, I met Nancy, who attended another university. We were married a year later, after we graduated from our respective schools.

After getting my MS at Penn State in 1968, Nancy and I headed to the University of Wisconsin – Madison, where I began work on my Ph.D. in Tree Physiology. Nearby Black Earth and Mount Vernon creeks were great laboratories for developing both fly design and angling concepts. While at Madison, Jason was born, and a couple of months after getting my Ph.D. in 1971, we moved as a family to Wausau, where I began my career as a professor at the University of Wisconsin – Marathon County.

In 1972 I sold my first magazine article—to "Field and Stream" magazine. A month later I became the Midwest Director for the Fenwick Fly Fishing Schools. That lead to extensive summertime travels as a family, teaching fly fishing across the country. On our initial trip to Montana, Jason caught his first trout on a fly rod. It was the start of a life-long fishing partnership between us.

During that decade, I also began to put some time into equipment design, with the first efforts yielding the Ultimate Wading Shoe. The success of that project encouraged me to continue design work whenever the opportunity presented itself.

I began writing regularly in the mid-1970s, and in 1979, Stackpole Press published my first book, *Nymphing*. That text was quickly followed by *Naturals* in 1981. It was also during the early 1980s that VCRs were starting to become a consumer commodity, and that lead to the filming of the 1982 video, *Nymphing*, produced in cooperation with my late friend, Mike Dry. The success of that video led to three more fly-fishing productions for the 3M Company shortly thereafter.

I spent much of the rest of the 1980s focusing on video production with my own company, but also continued to write, and published the *Borger Color System* during that time. In the background, Nancy and I created Tomorrow River Press, and in 1991, we published *Designing Trout Flies*. The book *Presentation* followed thereafter, in 1995.

Between those two projects, I had the chance to be involved in the film, *A River Runs Through It*, providing some time as a consultant. Since then, my fly-fishing efforts have been widespread, including work on DVDs, television shows, and eBooks.

Because of all those adventures in fly fishing, I have been blessed to have fished on every continent expect Antarctica. Even then, there are still so many places yet to visit—places where waters run cool and trout, steelhead, and salmon await my fly, and places where bonefish, permit and tarpon glide over impossibly blue flats. Yes, fly fishing still has many adventures waiting for me, and for all who call this matchless sport theirs.

For more info, visit: garyborger.com

About Jason

I grew up with fish, flies, and water. The summer of 1972 found our family on the banks of Montana's Squaw Creek. As my father surveyed the creek, he spotted the tell-tale flash of a nymphing fish. Handing me his rod, he pointed out the location and told me to cast. My two-handed, two-year-old compliance was not exactly graceful, but it put the fly where it needed to go. The fish moved again, my father shouted to set the hook, and soon I was clutching my first trout on a fly rod, a 13-inch rainbow. From that point on, fly fishing was always a part of my life.

As I grew up, I also got a formal education in fly-fishing, listening in as my father taught his angling schools across the country. Watching him teach instilled in me a desire to pursue fly fishing as a profession as much as a pastime.

My father published his first fly-fishing book, *Nymphing*, when I was nine years old. Seeing all of his long-hand and typewritten effort bound so neatly into 192 pages inspired me to want the same. Four years later, my first real article was published in "Fly Tyer" magazine. That article started me on the road to regular writing and illustrating.

Around the same time as that first "Fly Tyer" article, my father produced the now-classic instructional video, *Nymphing*. Seeing the 16mm cameras, the boom mics and the hotel-room dailies, I knew that I had to do something like that. My desires became reality in 1986, when my father and I hauled our Video-8 equipment out to Montana and shot *The Fabulous Bighorn*, the tape that kicked off the *Skills of Fly Fishing* series. Such productions continued through my high-school and college years, ultimately driving me to study film as my major.

My educational backgrounds in both fly fishing and film melded in 1991, when I worked on Robert Redford's silver-screen adaptation of Norman Maclean's novella, *A River Runs Through It*. The film brought me almost full-circle; the primary fishing-scene locations were only a few miles from where I caught my first-ever trout on Squaw Creek.

After *River*, I moved to Los Angeles to work full-time in the film and television industry. Some of the projects during that time involved fishing to a degree, and other projects, while far removed from angling, introduced me to good friends who also shared a passion for the fly. I loved my time working with film, but left L.A. after five years to pursue fly-fishing endeavors more deeply. Since my days in Los Angeles, my life has been focused on fly fishing in one way or another, including writing, video production and equipment design.

In 2002, my fly-fishing focus was broadened when I married my wife, Kelley. Kel also caught her first trout on a fly in Montana, and we said our vows on a mountainside near a rushing stream. Our lives together have seen many angling adventures, and my new-found role as Kel's "ghillie" has made being on the water even more of a pleasure.

Throughout my life, fly fishing has taken me to the most wild and beautiful places, and shown me the deeply involved rhythms of water, land, and fish. Fly fishing has been a way in which I could lose my sense of time, but also a way to challenge myself so intensely that a second ticked by like a carefully watched hour. Fly fishing has been with me as long as I can remember. Fly fishing is part of who I am.

For more info, visit: fishfliesandwater.com

The Books of the "Fly Fishing" Series

Below is a list of the 20 planned titles in the "Fly Fishing" series. They are projected to be released in the order shown, but as with all such undertakings, both titles and the release order may change. The series in slated to be completed in the 2015/2016 time-frame. You can keep up-to-date on the series at garyborger.com or fishfliesandwater.com.

Fishing the Film

Reading Waters

Long Flies

The Predatory Angler

Fly Gear

The Perfect Cast I

The Perfect Cast II

The Perfect Cast III

Nymphs & Wets

Terrestrials

Stillwaters

Spring Creek Particulars

Feathers, Fur, and Steel

Fly Designing

Really Matching the Hatch I

Really Matching the Hatch II

Favorite Flies & How We've Fished Them

Stream Strategies

The Compleat Fly Fisher

River of a Thousand Tongues

Index

D

E

F

Q

R

S

Z